WHAT PEOPLE ARE SAYING

"This book, The Storyteller's Mind Movie, is the gas pedal for entrepreneurs."

—Kevin Harrington, Best Selling Author, CEO of TVGOODS.com, Original Shark on SHARKTANK

"If you are looking to increase your ability to influence people and impact their hearts and minds, this is the book for you. This book will give you the most cutting-edge tools to do that."

—Kane Minkus, Founder/CEO of Industry Rockstars

"The Storyteller's Mind Movie is a book all sales and marketing teams and corporate leaders need to read and apply to their messaging."

—Marla Schimke, Head of Product Marketing, Broadcom

"I've known the power of storytelling in my own investor pitches---and to have this book now available for more entrepreneurs to shine in their own investor presentations is both welcomed and celebrated!"

—Caleb Carr, Founder/CEO/President, Vita Inclinata Technologies

"Your words and your visuals during an investor pitch are paramount. This book will help you stand out from the crowd so that your own business dreams come to fruition!"

—Amelia Marckworth, Director Innovation & Entrepreneurship Center, Seattle University

"The Storyteller's Mind Movie is terrific! It shows how to create human connection via story-telling in a fun, insightful and applicable way."

—Olia Kazenina, CEO of Mind Pattern LLC

"The Storyteller's Mind Movie by Melissa Reaves is a consumable and highly impactful how-to craft and tell impactful stories."

—Lisa L. Levy, Founder/CEO of Lcubed Consulting

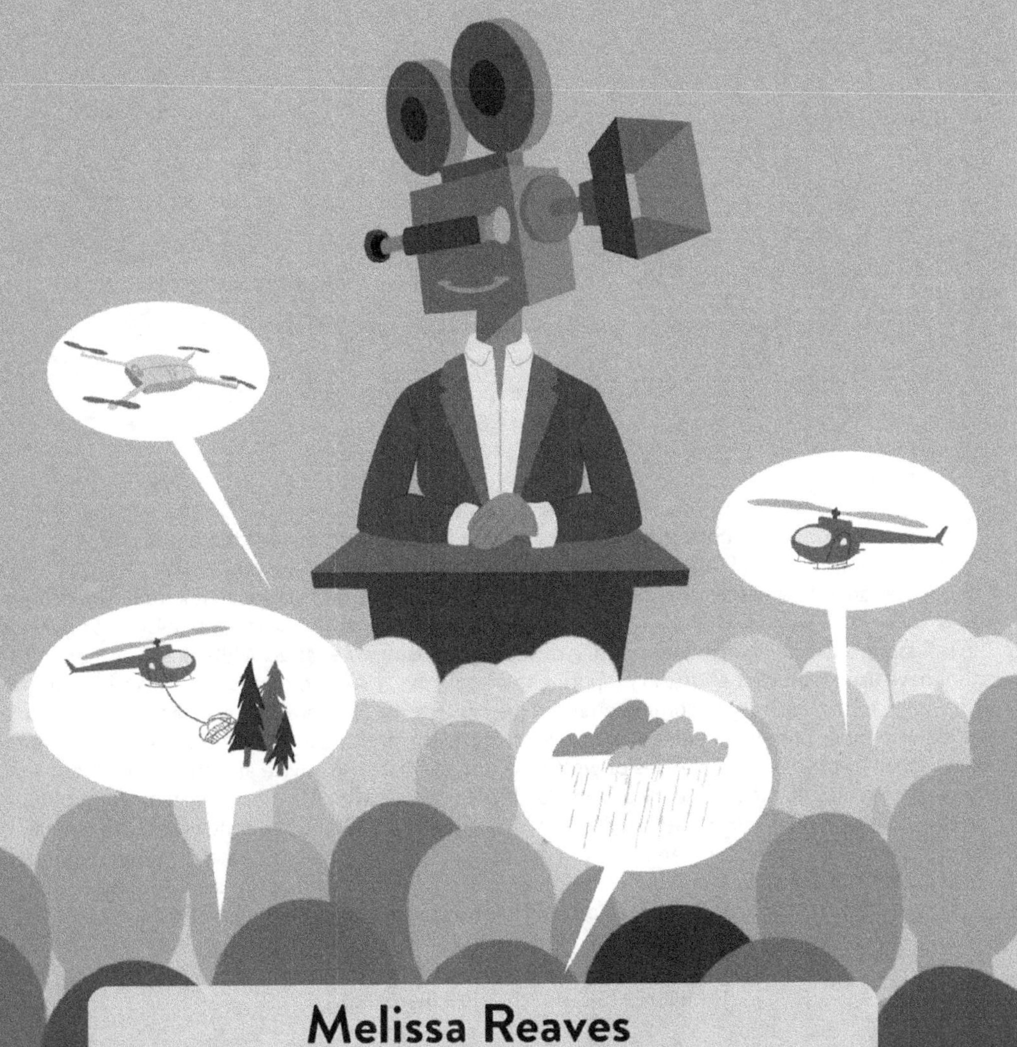

THE STORYTELLER'S MIND MOVIE
Become an Emotionally Connected Leader Through Your Storytelling Skills
"This book, The Storyteller's Mind Movie, is the gas pedal for entrepreneurs."
- Kevin Harrington, Original Shark on SHARKTANK
Melissa Reaves
CEO and Founder of Story Fruition

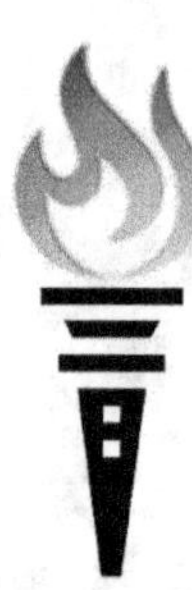

THE STORYTELLER'S MIND MOVIE
Become an Emotionally Connected Leader Through Your Storytelling Skills

Inspired Legacy Publishing is a division of (DBA) Inspired Legacy, LLC
PO Box 900816
Sandy UT 84090-0816.

ISBN 979-8-9872368-0-2 (paperback)
ISBN 979-8-9872368-1-9 (hardcover)

Printed in the United States of America.

CONTENTS

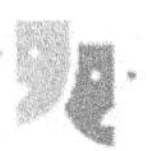

Process Six: Building Your Story Library - How to Organize Your Stories for Easy Access Both for Yourself, and Your Teams

FOREWORD BY LINDA FISK, CEO OF LEADHERSHIP GLOBAL, AUTHOR, TEDX SPEAKER

Melissa Reaves is a game-changing, revenue-building, performance-boosting change expert, and her new book, *The Storyteller's Mind Movie*, is an engaging and motivating read with practical and actionable insight based on real-world experience. Melissa showcases her profound public speaking and storytelling insight after spending years serving as a coach for executives and developing a reputation as a highly respected authority on the psychology of storytelling to create real action and impact.

In the current times, leaders need clear and simple direction and guidance to deal with unprecedented challenges, and actionable insight that helps them develop better outcomes and successful results. In clear and concise terms, Melissa explains how to present your case differently in order to get a different result. It has never been more critical for leaders to become more mindful, intentional, and knowledgeable on connecting with their employees, their shareholders, their investors, and their customers with confidence, in a rapidly changing world.

Let's face it, today, it's difficult to find a successful business that does not have a good story behind it. It's not enough to have a product or service that solves a problem - your company needs to stand out. Stories provide meaning, create context, and evoke a sense of purpose - and can captivate your audience – and Melissa's book tells you *how*. Storytelling is a strong business skill and when implemented effectively, it can boost a business in several ways, such as improving customer loyalty, creating a strong marketing strategy, increasing profit, and more. Storytelling conveys purpose - and businesses with purpose are noticed and win the loyalty of consumers. And that's the difference that Melissa Reaves offers.

This page-turner helps you use storytelling to help your audience to connect with you so they trust you - and your company. Melissa explains how to evoke emotions through storytelling and use the art and science of storytelling as a powerful tool to give your audience purpose and a motive to take action! *The Storyteller's Mind Movie* is the perfect balance of uplifting motivation and actionable takeaways. Importantly, after reading this engaging and enjoyable book, you'll learn to transfer your vision into a captivating story and clearly communicate it - to accelerate your success!

FIX THAT!
Caleb Carr's $300 Million Story Fruition

It's 2009, I'm fifteen years old and excited about the day. Today, I'm going to train to be a Search and Rescue professional, a dream I've had since I was six years old—and my trainer is a world-renowned expert. His name is Don and he's a cross between Sherlock Holmes and a bloodhound. If someone gets lost in a forest or on the side of a mountain, they send Don in to find them. He can read every twig break, grass motion, and clue to lead a team to the lost soul. He's found thousands of people in his career.

It's a rainy day in the Oregon area. Sideways rain, but I'm so eager to learn, it doesn't bother any of us in Don's troupe. We're about three miles into the forest when something happens. Don turns as pale as a ghost as he grabs his chest. He falls to his knees in pain, gasping for breath. One of our troupe members knows exactly what is happening: Don is having a heart attack! A troupe member immediately starts to administer CPR. Another member has a walkie-talkie and learns that a Blackhawk helicopter can be here in fifteen minutes.

Fifteen minutes is a long time for someone to be pumping your chest and blowing air into your lungs. I'm terrified.

The Blackhawk arrives. It's the first time I've ever seen one, let alone thirty feet above my head. The pilot's team is yelling down to us as they start to lower the rescue basket to Don. Our plan is we will hoist him up and take him to the hospital thirty miles away. But the wind and the trees want to play monkey-in-the-middle that day. The basket lowers, and the wind pushes it into the massive redwood trees. The 200-pound crewmen have to pull it back up and try again. The wind pushes the basket into what feels like the laughing trees again. Again. Same thing. Finally, the pilot has to make a hard call: *"We can't reach him. We have to abort this mission."*

Don died that day, ironically on the very mountain he had saved so many people himself. I guess the mountain wanted to keep him to herself that day.

Four years later, I'm in medical school when my professor asks, "Why do you want to go into medicine, Caleb?" I tell him the Don story. My professor pauses, and then simply says:

"Fix that. (Long pause) Don't let that happen again."

"What? What do you mean?" I ask.

"You have a lot of talented engineers in this school. Go find them and figure out how to fix that wind/basket problem."

So, I did. I assembled my team with Derek Sikora as lead engineer and we co-founded Vita Inclinata Technologies to design powerful drones that stabilize the rescue baskets anytime the winds aren't cooperating. Our technology is now purchased all over the world for military and industrial uses! We have offices in Denver, DC, and Dubai.

We get up every day to save lives with our technology.

Caleb Carr, Founder/CEO/President, Vita Inclinata Technologies, Denver/Washington, DC/Dubai

I heard Caleb's founder's story re-told to me after he won the Seattle University Business Plan competition (he's since won more). His story was so compelling that I became his fourth investor during the Family & Friends round of capital raising. I didn't look at a cap table or any business plan. It was *his powerful and vivid story* that got me so emotionally connected to his vision, so much so that I wrote a check. Vita Inclinata is now valued at over $300M and Caleb is still telling this story—among many others—as he travels his Vita Inclinata path. His natural storytelling skills help him be an *emotionally connected leader* as he balances his presentations with vivid storytelling and blending in data that is always needed in his work. That *Aha! Moment* is what gave me the inspiration to found Story Fruition LLC to help more business professionals shine like Caleb.

My life mission is to create millions of brilliant business storytellers who want to change the world.
Let that be you!

Melissa Reaves, Founder/CEO of Story Fruition LLC
Sammamish, WA

CHAPTER ONE

MY COMMITMENT TO YOU AND YOUR CAREER

Welcome. I'm thrilled to see you feeling compelled to pick up this book. I'm thankful because I hope it will change your life. And I hope after reading it, you are thankful. Thankful for taking on an **essential** business skill. A skill that is appreciated in the workplace and brings great hope to organizations. The storytellers in your company, including yourself, are the people that formulate the greatest connections with their audiences, staff, colleagues, clients, and investors. Congratulate yourself for picking this book up because it's fully intended to bring out the best in you as you expand your most important business skillset: **communication, connection, and human relations.**

Warren Buffet, an American business icon, who has amassed more personal wealth than most people think they could ever dream of, once said:

> *"Invest in yourself. The one easy way to become worth 50 percent more than you are (now at least), is to **hone your communication skills—**both written and verbal. If you can't communicate, it's like winking at a girl in the dark—nothing happens. You can have all the brainpower in the world, but you have to be able to transmit it. And the transmission is communication."*

Think about that. How you personally could become worth 50 percent more — and frankly, from what I've seen and experienced, his estimate is super conservative. When you read on, you'll discover why.

Storytelling is an enormously valuable skill to have because it makes humans relate to other humans in a variety of situations. Storytelling opens hearts so that we want to improve our business relationships, personal connections, and expand globally as we hear stories that inspire others to take action and buy new ideas, expand on existing processes, or bring solutions to something that once worked, but now appears stalled or broken. Storytelling is about living one life chapter at a time and reveling in your own storyline. You're the main character in your life, so capture it with your storytelling. Write them. Speak them. Sing them. Tell them. And tell them *well*!

This book is intended to improve your life. To help you realize your true potential as you allow your wisdom to be heard when you share it. To show your clients and colleagues, as well as your friends and family, that your stories are enriching, entertaining, poignant, rele-vant—and from your heart. Your audience will see that and—*that is magnetic*. That is mes-merizing. That is powerful.

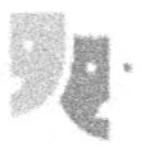

"The storyteller is the most powerful person in the world. The storyteller sets the vision values and agenda of an entire generation that is to come."
—Steve Jobs, CEO, Apple Corporation

WHY ARE STORYTELLERS SO POWERFUL?

You'll find out why as you continue into this book. If you follow what I teach, you'll change your life and greatly impact the lives of others.

You are about to go on an *adventure* because we are going to study the *science* and the *art* of storytelling and what it does with the listener's brain biochemically, and why that matters. You will also learn how to break down important life experiences where *you* changed as a result—that others will find valuable as lessons for their own lives.

Simon Sinek's powerful TEDx talk entitled "Start with Your Why" brilliantly shows us that people don't buy what you do, but *why* you do it. And how best to express that than through your storytelling skills that will inspire and uplift your staff, your clients, your partners, and followers? Take the time to find and craft your stories and watch your career catapult to new heights.

*"Because there are leaders and there are Those Who Lead. Leaders hold a position of power and authority. But Those Who Lead inspire us. Whether they're individuals or organizations, we follow Those Who Lead, not because we have to, but because we **want** to."*
—*Simon Sinek*

This is a hands-on guide not only to determine what your key stories are to sculpt for your own personal "Story Library," but also **how** to craft your stories so that they don't meander or sidetrack...or fumble!

"Not many of us were taught how to tell a story. In school, we were taught how to read a story, write a story, and analyze a story, but to master the oratory storytelling skills wasn't offered at many schools unfortunately. I'd like to change that and bring storytelling into the university level or sooner."
—*Melissa Reaves*

So, don't beat yourself up. As you hold this book, you are bravely stepping into exploring and honestly assessing your own skillsets and taking action to improve your leadership. That is a positive step forward in your career no matter how old, how young, or how "seasoned" you might be in life. **Pat yourself on the back.** You are about to amplify your own voice and get your message heard in ways that are concise, educational, entertaining, enriching, and even lucrative.

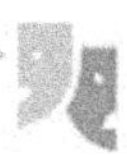

To take a positive step, you first stood in a negative place. From chaos comes clarity to find calmness—but as a storytelling student, you'll learn that the chaotic stage is where your story is being born! Many of my private clients start feeling embarrassed and deflated about their communication skills. In the first session, when they are about to learn core storytelling skills that will improve their careers, they are filled with anxiety.

- "I feel flat, and my audience looks limp."
- "I'm a pretty good storyteller, I think, because I'm fun at parties, but it's different when I'm at work. My nerves get the best of me."
- "I hate speaking in public. I get so nervous that I want to throw-up."
- "I know I'm losing my listeners by their glossy eyes as they check their phones. It's frustrating."
- "We have so much data to share, but then I see I'm drowning my audience with graphs and pie charts!"
- "The board wants me to say it a certain way, but I know deep down I could be painting the vision better and not sound so darn robotic."

Do any of those statements resonate?

YOU KNOW YOUR STUFF, BUT YOU…

- Fear you're boring your listeners and confusing your audience.
- Feel frustrated that the sales process is going much slower than expected, and your competition is eating your lunch.
- See disengagement across your organization because the team lacks inspiration, appreciation, and is not showing much loyalty on the job market. Does your retention feel like a revolving door?

Good news! This book will help you with your enhanced communication skills, point you right towards Warren Buffet's "50 percent more" in success and net worth—and from what we're seeing- so much more in your lifetime!

If you currently believe that you don't have any stories or that when you tell a story it's boring and takes too long to tell or is told too quickly and doesn't get the emotional reaction you were hoping for, then this book will show you how to:

- **Create an easy story** arc *every time* you tell it that is entertaining and exciting.
- **Deliberately create "Mind Movie" images** so that your listener can see it, touch it, taste it, smell it, *feel* it, and *buy*_it! Stories *sell* and everyone sells *something*. It could be your product, service, vision, idea, and solutions. As the storyteller, you hold a lot of power, so use it joyfully and wisely.
- **Empower your voice, body expression, pace, and tones** to let the audience know how the characters in your stories feel about each other. How they choose to like or dislike a character you're talking about. That's pure entertainment! High five, Storyteller!

- **Compose powerful visual presentations** that support your words and your overall story. This is where many presenters fumble because they include too much copy that overwhelms the audience and loses their interest. This book will show you how to keep the communication train on the tracks and not derail. **Build your own "Story Library" of key moments in your life.** You have Stories of Resilience; Stories of Bravery; Stories of Triumph: Stories of a Mess Up. All of them make you who you are as a leader, and therefore bring your leadership forward as multifaceted and invigorating, because your stories show how human you are—and how human your audience is as well.

WHY HAVE A STORY LIBRARY?

Your own Story Library can be pulled out brilliantly when you're on:

- A podcast as a guest
- A podcast as a host
- A panel receiving live questions from audience members

Your Story Library will be your best friend while presenting your leadership and expertise at a:

- **Capital raising meeting** and your investor pitch deck *must* shine your message *crystal clear* to get those millions of dollars your start-up needs. If this *vital* slide presentation doesn't tell your vision, your STORY, you will leave money on the table. Every page tells a story that can fund your company when told effectively in both words and images. More on this later in the book.
- **Boardroom meeting** updating the members on your quarterly successes or challenges—so that everyone sees your vision and rapport with all situations.
- **Town halls** and you want your team and the entire company to feel appreciated and inspired or calm during choppy waters. Your personal stories will open their hearts—and you biochemically and intentionally made that happen. *Hello oxytocin. Welcome to my storytelling. Welcome to my leadership.*
- **Ted Talks, TEDx** or *any* stage that has a big red dot and a microphone and cameras. Congratulations! That is such an exciting and career game-changer—so make it: Amazing. Connected. Clear. Educational. Entertaining.
- **Officiate of a wedding** or a Celebration of Life. Your storytelling soothes hearts as joyous memories are shared.
- **Interview situations** and are being asked questions that you can share your own personal wisdom that reflect your character. Stories of Resilience. Stories of Overcoming Obstacles. Stories when you were the Hero. Stories of when you felt like the Zero. Stories of when you closed the most zeroes!
- **Dating and marriage improvement.** Yep, even in your most personal relationships, storytelling skills matter—so these skills easily cross over to every area of your communication. When you can entertain your significant other by sharing personal moments that show *all-of-who-you-are* and how you see the world, well, that's just sexy, Storyteller!

And also if you're a parent or grandparent, then your ability to communicate family "stories" to solidify your family history is now part of your legacy. Telling these stories keeps your family lineage alive.

Each key *aha!* event in your life offers lessons, and that lesson can only be communicated through the story of it. What happened? How old were you in this story? Who were you with? And as you read and practice this book, you'll know how to precisely project that into the minds of your listeners as they create a real-time "Mind Movie" with your every word and delivery skills. And this book is committed to getting you there.

Now as we move forward, I have a Double-Dog-Dare-You-Challenge.

If you're reading this as a physical book:

**HIGHLIGHT THIS BOOK, WRITE IN IT, EARMARK IT
AND PLEASE...
READ IT AGAIN.**

I hope you delight in answering the story prompts that spark memories of your triumphs and tribulations. Create a journal where you can keep the seeds of your stories in one place and it's for your eyes only. In fact, to support you, we have created a companion journal especially designed to help you discover your stories and build your storytelling library. (Just look in the back of this book at the resource section to learn more about it and additional resources that can support your journey.) I hope you feel invigorated crafting the story so that it's so vivid that everyone who hears it feels the emotional impact you felt. As they connect more to you as a human, the easier it is for them to trust your vision and buy in.

If you're also listening to this Audio book, kudos! Reading and listening to this material deepens your comprehension of the life-changing material. The more ways you find to bring in all of your senses and multiple formats (reading, listening, visioning, journaling) to support you on the journey, the more you will gain from this powerful information.

The Eyes and Ears Working Together —Lock It In!

In fact, I highly recommend listening to the audio version because this will actually let you **hear** other business professionals like you tell their stories using my Story Fruition, Mind-Movie approach. This is primarily a story-*telling* focus, so the audio brings all the core concepts to life as you listen to our voice inflections to vividly create clear characters with a steady story arc that is enjoyable to follow. And, if you want to be on podcasts, you only have your words and voice inflections to create the Mind Movies in the listeners—so the audio version of this book will catapult your grasp and understanding of the teachings.

As you **re-read this book** and start to answer some of the prompts, may you reapproach all your presentations using a Mind Movie Maker perspective. Ask yourself, *How can my*

presentation tell the story for our potential investors, clients, or partners and alliances? And, how to make deck tell our story even if I'm not there to tell it?

I want you to delight in the realization that your stories are powerful and impactful. That when you share your wisdom, your foolery, your humbling—your **vulnerability**—that you realize, **truly** realize—that you are a valuable person who matters and your stories matter.

So, let's find *your* stories. Craft them. Decorate them. And make them delicious to tell—and hear—for all parties.

BRINGING A STORY TO FRUITION

This book is dedicated to the creative entrepreneurs, leaders, decision makers, "Rising Stars," and business visionaries in our world who awake each day with a goal to change and improve our lives. Some are fixing systems and processes that are broken; or expanding them because they are ready; they may be bringing something significant forward that no one has produced or thought of yet. They tap into the vast, unlimited power of our human imagination and retrieve stories for us to utilize for the collective good of humankind. They help us create better lives for all.

All kinds of entrepreneurs, visionaries, and business leaders have stories that brought them to these transformational moments. If you are an inventor or salesperson, you know you have stories too! If you are any business professional, you definitely have a library of stories that span your career and lifetime. Doctors, lawyers, teachers, realtors, bankers, software engineers, accountants, scientists, community leaders, parents, and healers all have stories. Interesting stories, but they just don't know how to tell them like they mean them to be received. This book will help you recognize which stories are worth spending your time developing, and how each story, when crafted and delivered well, will move your audience in the direction your idea is going.

SO, WHAT'S *YOUR* STORY?

We will explore your Founder's Story, or what I term your "Story Fruition." We'll look at personal experiences that have taught you valuable lessons that you can use in your career and leadership roles to express to others. And we'll look at customer success stories because these stories are told by your sales and marketing teams and your C-Suite. Every member of your organization needs to be well-trained in storytelling because your customers respond differently when they encounter a great storyteller during any presentation. And the Storytellers leave the competition far behind. They use storytelling to communicate their organization's why. And as Simon Sinek says, "People don't buy what you do, but why you do it."

This book will also cover the visuals within a presentation that support and amplify the golden thread of your story – the point, the reason for *why* you are there, so that your listeners are engaged and remember you. Drawing on all my years of experience, I can assure you that your audience will retain your story far longer than any pie chart! The visuals *support* this process and help you *tell* your story, but as you will see, they are *not* the story. Being intentional with every decision you make in your presentation, taking conscious control of what data you choose to include—and what you choose to leave out—so that you're not overwhelming the listener to the point where they disengage, is a *crucial* part of the artform of business storytelling. These decisions will make or break your idea.

Thank you for taking the time to look more closely at traditional storytelling that we all know so well. Storytelling that has been seen on countless stages across the globe and is now being taken into boardrooms, keynote stages, and sales meetings. Enhance your skills and make your stories have great impact.

Stories matter. Stories sell. And the storyteller has *all* the power—and even more importantly, the *obligation* to educate and entertain and inspire your listeners. This book will show you how to take your story from a misplaced, meandering set of experiences into a captivating, vivid Storyteller's Mind Movie.

Ready to mesmerize your audiences? Let's go! Your life is a real page turner.

CHAPTER TWO

MY OWN STORY FRUITION

I started acting at the ripe old age of nine, studied theater at the University of Michigan, and became a professional improviser at fifty, so I've been studying the art of storytelling for almost (*gulp*) five decades. Guess what? It works. My company, Story Fruition LLC, has helped generate over $70M in investment money to flow into the American economy and ignite the dreams of founders who want to change the world just in the last few years alone.

I was able to get here because my over twenty-year technology sales career at the enterprise level, which included clients and employers of Oracle, Microsoft, Cisco, Best Buy, and countless advertising agencies seeking technical solutions for their digital marketing needs—made me tell stories. Case studies, or what I deem "Case Stories," were how we navigated towards success.

Today, I teach business professionals, founders, C-Suite executives, and "Rising Star" managers all over the world how to tell better stories to bolster their careers, build their customer connections, secure capital funding, and grow revenue. But it wasn't always this way...and now I will share my own vulnerability with you...

PINK SLIP TO BLISS

It's a cold January 2nd, and I'm angry. I'm crying. I'm furious because I've just been brutally fired from a job—that I can't stand. Apparently, my distress working for this company had been heard by the Universe, for it answered me with a pink slip.

To add to the stress I am experiencing, one of my children is having health issues, which requires a lot of time and care. I feel it is a requirement to find a new high-paying tech job. In the past, these roles always came with lots of travel, where I'd be gone for several days each month, pitching and servicing Fortune 500 companies with their ad technology.

I have been a top sales producer for most of my career, but as ad tech continues to expand, it has become more complicated and overcrowded. Thousands of industry logos showing the ad tech eco-system are overwhelming to stand out from the crowd, even as I sit at one of the top technologies. Puppy start-ups are nipping at my heels and I just want to kick them away. We quibble for pennies based on the conversion the ad could be attributed to—and many cheat at it. The space is getting ugly, and I am tired of it. Sunday night's anxiety catapults as

I have five more long days ahead tending to something that no longer brings me joy other than the paycheck.

This *I-no-longer-care-about-your-click-through-rate* disdain is showing up in my interviews with ad tech companies too. I am struggling to hide my actual panic and desperation in my interview—and that is not an attractive feature in any candidate. I think they can smell it on me. I am scared, tired, worried about my child, and getting my derriere kicked on the job market. My ego is getting hammered. I am crashing. I'm terrified.

In addition, the new generation of hiring managers are now young thirty-somethings— usually named *Ryan-Bryan-or-Erik* – (same guy, different body, similar plaid lumberjack shirt; This is Seattle after all). And they are nimbler with ad tech because they have been holding a computer mouse since they were born, versus *my* first computer mouse experience at the University of Michigan's engineering lab when I was twenty years old back in the 1980s. I am biologically old enough to be Ryan-Bryan-or-Erik's mom. And I know I am not going to go to the sports bars and talk Seahawks or soccer with them. I don't even own a TV.

I HAVE A PROBLEM I NEED TO SOLVE.

I often like to have conversations with my **Gut Instinct** from time to time.. It is that voice that knows better. Everyone has one and probably has learned through trial and error not to ignore it. It's profound and always has led me to the right path—except when I chose to ignore it and go in a different direction from my gut, (which I did when I took on this terrible job that just kicked me to the curb heartlessly.) But that was then.

Now, my inner friend, Gut Instinct, is leading me to the right place when I ask important questions or am struggling with any decision. The conversations go something like this:

Me: Really? Fired? But I need the salary!

Gut Instinct: Um, no....You need to find *joy*. You need to find your true essence and embrace it.

Me: But I don't have talents beyond what I've been doing. And (sigh), that does not bring me a charge anymore.

Gut Instinct: Agreed. That's why you got the pink slip. You're welcome!

Me: You're welcome? I'm not sure I'm feeling very grateful yet.

Gut Instinct: You'll get there. Next... Learn to quiet your mind and just listen to us more. We'll guide you. Trust.

Me: Trust? Okay. Who am I talking to again?

Gut Instinct: You're listening to your higher self. Good for you! The world gets better the more people do listen to their own Gut Instinct. What you are about to create, Melissa, is extraordinary. Keep listening to us.

Me: Whatever. Okay.

This no-good-very-bad day leaked into bad weeks, which flooded into financially a painful couple of years. My credit card was my key source to live on, and I racked up $50K in debt. *When will the hemorrhaging stop?*

Crisis usually brings out the most self-reflection for change to occur. During this particular *wheels-in-mud-spinning-endlessly* moment, I consciously and deliberately dive deep down into the dirt of my situation and will figure out how I magnetized this mess (because I have), and now, *What do I really want to do? What STORY am I living through right now? Who are the characters? How do I feel about them? Why should anyone care?*

Me: Hey, Gut Instinct, what would bring me joy? This is my life after all, and I'm the captain of my fate and the master of my Soul, according to *Think and Grow Rich*! So, tell me, please!

Gut Instinct: Always listening to *you*…let it out…

Me: What brings me joy AND could also provide an income? Sure, I want to be happy with what I do, but I also want a great lifestyle. I want my two children to see their mom bounce back after the divorce and be better and stronger than ever. I want to delight clients with what I have to bring to help them strive towards their own goals and *thrive* when they get there. What is it that I could do?

Gut Instinct: Go make a list of what you are good at and what brings you joy.

I obey Gut Instinct and I open a notebook and begin to write a list of what I've learned and gained during my life and my career:

WHAT BRINGS ME JOY?

1. *I have over twenty-five years of very successful advertising tech sales and marketing experience.*
2. *I'm always a top producer.*
3. *I'm fast on my feet due to all my improv training—and that works great in business!*
4. *Very little "shakes me," as I've learned to just go with the flow and have fun using my improv moxie.*

5. *I've worked at many software start-ups and know how important it is to paint the vision story for early adopters to jump into.*

6. *I know case studies can help close deals; the trick is how you tell them. I know most salespeople do not do a great job at delivering them due to a lack of training. Telling someone else's story takes work. That's where my acting abilities come in handy!*

7. *I have learned how to synthesize information– to take multiple pieces of data flying out of various people's mouths at the same time and make it into something clear and vivid.*

8. *I know how to edit and have a good visual understanding for presentations.*

9. *I've been doing some cool things with the Seattle University Business Plan Competition contestants, teaching them to infuse stories into their presentations. The feedback I'm getting is super positive.*

10. *I love entrepreneurs! I appreciate the way they start with an idea and then let it grow until it comes to fruition!*

11. *I know a lot of business professionals hate public speaking but know they have to do it on various levels every day – and they love it when I coach them—and I love it too.*

This list makes me feel better. I feel proud of my talents and decide to let things unfold naturally. Relax and allow the flow of things to direct me to the next chapter of my career. *"Everything is going to work out,"* I say. Or is that my Gut Instinct saying it to me?

A couple of days later, my dear friend, Kent Whipple, offers his wonderful storytelling class at Unexpected Production in Seattle. This is an awesome place where I've been doing professional improv for years, and I leap at the chance to study with him. I have no idea why because I am pretty fulfilled with improv, but Gut Instinct says, "Take his class!"

KENT CHANGES MY LIFE.

We meet on Saturdays for two and a half hours at our improv theater, where Kent teaches us how to construct our stories. He shares prompts and exercises that pull out precious moments when I felt an Aha! of understanding the lesson learned. My brain is on fire! Stories are pouring out of me in every class—and even my first drafts are powerful because of my acting and improv skills. I love the process of improving each story as I play with my characters and dialogues. My joy is now exploding!

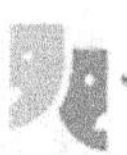

To conclude the class, we perform one of our stories in front of a live audience. He teaches us how to adjust the mic, stay close to it, and make sure to connect with all angles of the audience so that they feel included. I tell "The Santa Game" as my story. I play the village idiot in this story and the audience is cracking up. Just as I step off stage, Kent turns to me. "Melissa, I think you just found your new medium."

I gasp. Kent is absolutely right! I *am* a storyteller!

Gut Instinct somehow knows that the one decision to take a class when I was down, out, poor, and stressed eventually—and essentially—leads me to finding my Self.

TO BE A GOOD STORYTELLER, YOU MUST DO THE WORK.

As my skills and my own Story Library grows, I realize that to master *anything* you have to **study it, practice it, and teach it**. I refer to that as a Mastership Trifecta.

I return to my notebook and review my list of talents and interests again. *Could I somehow blend all my sales, marketing, acting, AND my storytelling skills into my ideal job?*

I have clearly seen the need in the corporate meetings. My eyes water while droning managers flash endless graphs, charts, and words on a slide. The presentations aren't holding my attention, and I see my colleagues zoning out, too, as they scroll their phones or look out the window. "The Problem" is the presenter more than anything.

And then the ultimate question hit me. Would *people <u>pay</u> me to help them shine in their business and investor pitch presentations by teaching them storytelling?*

As I ponder whether I should start my own consulting company, I instantly hear and feel you know who...

Gut Instinct: Yes. Yes, they will pay you. They will hire you. *Take a leap of faith* as this is something you've wanted since you were twenty-five years old. You forgot, but now you're remembering. This is your Life's path, Melissa. Step boldly onto it. We've got you.

And so, on that ordinary April day, Story Fruition LLC was born at my kitchen table in Sammamish, Washington. And I've never looked back. I experience joy with all my clients and amazing projects that come my way. Friendships formulate because the work we do together is not just fun—but is also meaningful. When I see a client hear their own Story Fruition played back to them using my Mind Movie techniques, many have heartwarming tears rolling down their face.

"I've never heard my own story told like that before.... it's beautiful. It's MY story, as I lived it, and I could see it clearly when you told it.... wow....Teach me how to do that!"
Jim Hardwick, Founder/Executive Director, Magnificent Significance
—Chandler, Arizona

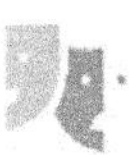

GO WITH THE FLOW

After formulating Story Fruition, I immediately start crafting an interactive workshop called, "Storytelling for Business Professionals." Tickets are flying and I'm seeing referrals in all the subsequent ones. Students love it! Most are understanding my process, and the few who struggle with parts of it, are data feedback so that I can improve my lessons. I see my process is working in the business realm.

Me: *Wait, I have a process?*

Gut Instinct: *YES. You have a process that's fun to follow. KEEP GOING!*

Me: *Yes sir! Sir? Ma'am?...*

Gut Instinct: *We're nonbinary.*

What I see now, as I look at my own Story Fruition, is that I was entering what I'd describe as the *Entrepreneur's Dream State* that day I opened that notebook and started writing freely about what brings me joy. To let myself simply daydream without resistance, and to actively listen for Gut Instinct to shine the light on my next step on my path has been my own adventure.

AND NOW, YOU'RE STEPPING ONTO YOUR OWN ADVENTURE.

What I love about entrepreneurs and business leaders and visionaries is that they don't see, or even accept, the "reality" world that most of us see. An entrepreneur or visionary will dream how to make something better. Drifting off into their imagination, gently asking and exploring an idea without pressure on it...*Why do it **that** way, when I could do it **this** way? That's much easier. What if others feel that way, too?*

THE ENTREPRENEUR'S DREAM STATE IS WHEN THE STORY IS REALIZED.

That is when the dream is born and that is when you step onto the path to improve the world! So, tell *that* story, and perhaps you'll have a $300 Million Story Fruition, like Caleb Carr too. And he's not the only one. What is your dream? How do you plan to change the world? This is about you. Your story. Your business and organization. Your relationships. Your bank accounts. Your Story Fruition. Isn't it time to seize?

So, grab your notebook and buckle up, for you are in for the adventure of your life!

PROCESS ONE
STORY MINING

HOW TO FIND YOUR STORIES AND WHAT TO DO WITH THEM

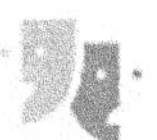

CHAPTER THREE

REAPPROACHING "THE PROBLEM / SOLUTION" MODEL

Many times a week, I hear new clients say, "I don't have any stories really. I have a few I tell, but most of the time, I think my stories are boring." My heart saddens when I hear this because it couldn't be further from the truth. You are a walking story machine! All day, every day there are stories being played out; moments explaining past stories that you've not come to peace with yet; and when you daydream, you're writing a story of your future. It's your Vision Story—and then you get to watch it unfold. Your life is a page turner.

What we're going to do in this section is show you how some clients found their stories, and you'll be given prompts and instructions on how to allow your Creative Flow to come through without you getting in the way of it. This is key. **Let the story come out.**

Here's a story of when I first learned to story-mine from a client.

BREAK IT, REBUILD IT

It's a cloudy March Day in Seattle. Spring is thinking about waking up, but the lavender crocus flowers have not yet decided to pop out of the ground to let us know that our winter nap is about over. I walk into a small conference room on the Seattle University's campus. I'm greeted by seven business school students who are representing three different companies for the annual Harriett Stephenson Business Plan competition. They will be battling it out for a $10,000 prize to turn their dreams into entrepreneurial reality. High stakes on the table.

I'm a volunteer pitch coach.

The previous year, I had seen the competition and watched as the nervous presenters shared in two-minute "Fast Pitches" on how they would change the world. Overall, the presentations were data and analytical leaning. Facts, percentages, logic, and generalities. Nothing that grabbed us to invest – emotionally or otherwise. I'm standing next to Amelia Marckworth, one of the Seattle University directors that hosted the competition. Amelia loves an entrepreneurial spirit and is held in high regard in our city for connecting people in the start-up space—and at just thirty years old, this woman gets it done. We have that in common, and from the second we met, I knew our friendship would blossom like spring crocus flowers.

As I watch the presenters struggle to emotionally connect their audience to their ideas, I turn to her and lightly punch her in the arm, "How can I help next year? I know I can improve these pitches! We can make them better storytellers like what we saw with Vita Inclinata last year!" I then start to rattle off my resumé of over twenty years in sales, marketing, ad tech —

"And I'm a professional improviser! I write stories on the fly all the time. These students need stories associated to these pitches. I promise this will work."

"Okay," she says. "But I need to listen to this year's contest right now."

"Oh. Right. Sorry...."

Almost nine months later, the phone rings, and it's Amelia.

"We would love to have you join this year's competition to help with the pitches. I liked your idea about adding the storytelling into their presentations. You still game?"

"Am I still game? Absolutely! Let's do this," I say.

As I sit myself down in the conference room, the students smile and share who their teams would consist of. Two Nigerian partners that had an idea about helmet safety for cyclists, because in Africa, bikes are one of the most utilized forms of transportation, and helmet safety isn't promoted enough. "We see helmets as opportunities for custom works of art to inspire people to wear them for fashion as much as safety," shares the woman. I think, *What a creative idea!*

"Tell me about your idea," I ask. She starts with a graph that says, "Problem: Helmet safety is a problem in Africa," and then immediately starts throwing facts and figures at me about the stats of helmet injuries and the death toll. Her male partner holds up the stats, graphs, and pie charts. All data. No emotional connection to a highly emotional problem that literally centers around life-or-death outcomes. It is a good idea filled with heart and human care.

Me: But how could a pie chart communicate the power of her true mission?

Gut Instinct: It can't.

The second business plan competition team has four members, comprised of two women and two young men. They observed that the coffeehouses of Seattle are a *goldmine* for urban gardening. Coffeehouses are everywhere because most Seattleites need high-octane caffeinated beverages to wake up and focus because we've been up all-night engineering companies like Microsoft, Amazon, Nordstrom, Alaska Airlines. *Yea, we think a lot in Seattle. Must be the rain.*

The team's idea presented how we could be more environmentally sustainable by taking the used coffee grounds and converting them into powerful plant fertilizer and even fuel. Again, a woman took charge, which I found refreshing because in the ad-tech space I had grown up in, I was outnumbered by primarily males who all vied for the biggest piece of the ad-tech pie. *So, you go, ladies!*

Carrie, one of the women on the team, starts explaining "The Problem" in the exact same way as the Helmet Team did, by immediately flinging a lot of numbers and confusing graphs to illustrate the amount of coffee ground waste that is accumulated each day, each week, each month. Then she said, "'The Solution' is our method: to take used coffee grounds and convert them into garden fertilizer. The 'Addressable Market' is the urban dweller, primarily women aged twenty-five to fifty-five."

NO PHOTOS. ALL GRAPHS. NO EMOTIONAL CONNECTION.

"Carrie...let's talk about women aged twenty-five to fifty-five—-so if you're twenty-four or fifty-six, forget about it? How does age really play into your target market? Can't anyone who is a conscious consumer benefit from buying your product? What does your customer value? How do they try to live their daily lives? Are they conscientious to the greater good? Or do they think recycling is for tree huggers?"

They stare at me. They slowly start to put their pie charts down as they realize that their presentation isn't offering an emotional or relatable connection. It was only logical data; it didn't evoke true emotional connection—and they need to balance it out.

The energy of the room starts shifting. We are going somewhere new and inspired together; to a place where pitches are logical *and* emotional. "That's how people buy—if it makes sense, and makes them feel good, hopeful, relieved, accomplished, and a part of something positive—they'll keep buying. And it's the STORY of that customer journey – from problem to solution – that will sell the product. Not the product on its own. People using your product and seeing their lives change for the better is the gamechanger," I share.

Smiles appear across their faces. Light bulbs over their heads are illuminating.

The third company is a solo-preneur named Daniel. He has a warm smile that compliments his red hair. "I'm a woodworker. My company strives to connect quality furniture buyers with artisan furniture makers."

Then Daniel does the exact same thing, "The Problem: Approximately 43 percent of people polled about the quality of their furniture are not happy...."

Aha!

I realize right then and there that I have a purpose to change the way the entrepreneur pitch, or any business presentation, could go in order to instantly connect the listener to their mission.

Let's emotionally tie their idea to a business narrative! I want to show them *how* to create a story with characters having the problem. Make *the company* the hero who offers the solution.

Let's create a *Mind Movie* so that when the speaker is done, the audience knows *exactly* what is intended to change the world. The listeners can see, hear, smell, taste, and feel your vision. You're deliberately creating their Mind Movie and that is now edu-tainment! Imagine seeing the audience's heads nodding with excitement, ready to ask questions, instead of them scratching their heads because they feel overwhelmed with a massive data-dump!

"Daniel, let's look at this a little closer... Putting the facts and figures to one side for a moment, tell me about the 'Artisan Woodworkers' so we're clear on this character."

He lights and says, "Well, I'm an artisan woodworker. I work out in the garage, mostly on the weekends, because I have PTSD from serving in Iraq. Woodworking relaxes me."

"First, thank you for your service. We appreciate your dedication to our country."

He smiles, "You're welcome."

I continue, "And great that you are your own core target market. Tell me what you like about woodworking?"

Daniel then effortlessly describes the smell of the sawdust, the smoothness of the wood that has been sanded down from its rougher beginnings, but the moment he starts to describe putting stain on the virgin white wood and guiding it to its new shade, Daniel lights up. And, in that moment, Daniel became not just a national hero, but our business narrative's hero too.

"So, tell me about your customer? Who will be buying these pieces of furniture art?" I ask.

A robotic, business-school response follows. "Women aged twenty-five to fifty-four, making a HHI of $75K," he replies.

"Daniel, what does a fifty-four-year-old woman have in common with a twenty-five-year-old woman other than the fact that they both probably know how to cook a meal? Tell me about her—her state of furniture affairs and what she values. Does she have furniture that's come out of a box and there are extra pieces lying around that weren't used?"

He laughs. "Yes...probably. We see them coming out of the IKEA stage."

Then BOOM. I realize that *I* was his target market back in my late twenties. I shared my story.

PAINT A PICTURE AT THE BEGINNING.

I'm twenty-seven-years old and selling advertising space for an L.A. Weekly newspaper. It was a great day job because it allowed me to do some auditions — I had moved to L.A. to find out whether I wanted to be a professional actor. I dream to be on sitcoms or maybe a soap opera. So, selling ads pays the bills better than waiting tables for me. I am the Melrose rep and get to call on all the "hip and happening" shops of L.A. in the West Hollywood territory. I walk door

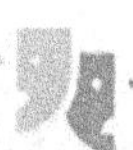

to door in my cool maroon Doc Martens, a trendy sundress, and a leather motorcycle jacket calling on a slew of restaurants, record shops, comic bookstores, bars, and furniture stores. In my mind, *I am the BOSS!*

THE INCITING EVENT

One afternoon, I walk into a store on Third Avenue. It smells of pine and furniture varnish. The furniture is stunning, and all built by a first-generation immigrant from Mexico, Jefe. He barely speaks English and relies on his store manager to translate, but what he lacks in communication with me, he more than makes up for in talent. His style is the perfect cross between 'shabby and chic,' or the Pottery Barn style that is all the rage. I go nuts imagining all of his furniture in my apartment with my newlywed husband. We buy a pine armoire, a queen-size sleigh bed, two end tables, a dining room table, and six chairs. Jefe agrees to design my desk for work! *Things are getting fancy at our place!*

Friends walk into our apartment- and bear in mind that we were all in our twenties, still using milk crates for TV stands, along with our IKEA purchases-and they are stunned. *"You look like adults!"* they say. And we *feel* like adults. Our place looks like a home. And it makes me proud to host parties and just feel the success I am experiencing in my early-stage sales career.

That's when I knew that *furniture could turn your house into a castle-* aesthetically and emotionally!

WHY A STORY?

Daniel composed a story using these frameworks and personas to connect to his audience because we are humans, and humans demand connection. As he stepped onto that stage two weeks later, in an auditorium filled with an audience of three hundred of Seattle's top angel investors there to scout the brightest minds in the country, he told them his story, and he *owned* it. He had rehearsed this moment and felt solidly comfortable with the journey he was going to take his audience on for the next three minutes.

"It's been a long day. You've just arrived home and you're tired. All you can think about is putting your feet up and enjoying a beverage to help you relax into the evening. You look around your home and see the beautiful custom-made coffee table—and you smile. You feel that the success you've dreamt of is a reality- you're no longer looking at *starter furniture,* the boxy table—you pulled out of a box—and assembled with Swiss instructions. Your home, is indeed, your castle. Quality, artisanal furniture makes you feel like a king (or queen) in your own home," he opens.

While Daniel presented, I could hear the people behind me in the audience whisper, "Fred, that reminds me of our coffee table from your grandmother. It's so beautiful and well made!"

When your audience starts to tell their own stories sparked from your story...then you know that you're moving the decision wheel in the right direction. There's no better compliment from your audience than if they temporarily see images, people, or places that they connect to because of your powerful words as the Storyteller.

As humans, we connect with stories far faster and longer than any graph or pie chart. When people walk away after hearing your pitch, presentation, or keynote, they are going to associate your brand with the story far longer than your Cap Table details. Don't get me wrong, those elements are important—investors and customers buy logically, but please don't ever underestimate the power of emotion. Find your story and lead with it. When you compose your story that's gently infused with relevant data to back it up, you'll lock into your listeners' memory better than any pie chart could ever hope to do.

OUR BRAIN ON STORY

The brain is a complicated and beautiful organ that acts a lot like a computer. It's constantly taking in data, analyzing how the data makes us feel on an emotional level, and then outputting beliefs, opinions, and decisions. We rely on our brains to operate everything from telling us that we're thirsty or hungry, to making quick decisions like speeding up to beat the yellow light before it turns red, to just walking, one foot in front of the other, without paying conscious attention to the behavior itself. Our brain has that on autopilot.

God love ya, Brain. You are hugely appreciated.

The brain also uses data to form opinions and make decisions on whether to act on or pass on opportunities. When we flash a graph at someone, the neocortex of our head noodle engages. We see the lines and graphs, the words...we are reading the slide, but we are not fully engaging or even necessarily experiencing *feelings* about what we are seeing. It's rational and logical.

When we add a story to our presentations, we power-surge the limbic portion of our brain that ignites images and emotions through the driving force of neurotransmitters like oxytocin, dopamine, and endorphins, all rapidly firing off and illuminating your brain in technicolor, pulling you into a time and space dimension (of the storyteller's choosing) through their words, their voice tonalities, and their body language. The limbic system has a big say in our behavior, but it doesn't compute in words, but rather in feelings. It drives our decision-making and our memories, so when it hears and feels an emotionally rich story before an analytical graph—you now are putting "Heart in The Chart." So, why wouldn't you make sure to fire that part of the brain up when you're aiming to win someone's favor?

Please read that paragraph again.

*"Narratives are easier to process and generate more attention and engagement
[for the brain than] traditional, logical-scientific communication."*
—Michael F. Dahlstrom, PhD, Science Communication, Iowa State University

PIE CHARTS DON'T EVOKE OXYTOCIN OUT OF THE GATE

I highly recommend that you watch a TED Talk by David JP Phillips titled, "The Magical Science of Storytelling." He does a brilliant job of showing us how to deliberately infuse the brain with neurotransmitters to get the *exact* emotional reaction you seek. For example, if you are a non-profit organization that helps homeless teens find housing and it's time to fundraise, you'll want to introduce an oxytocin-laced story that invokes generosity, trust, and bonding. Empathy through your story will help you achieve this. Tell a story about one of your beneficiaries who was down and out, get into the details of their plight, take your time, and watch the oxytocin kick into your audience's heads. When it's time to ask whether they'll support your cause, there's a far greater likelihood of you getting a YES from a story than an analytical graph of teen homelessness.

In his TED Talk, Phillips goes on to show how dopamine-laced stories summon focus and motivation to take action because you've introduced a cliffhanger into your story: the intentional suspense as your listeners perch on the edge of their seats, anticipating the next moment, longing to hear how this story ends. Imagine if a CEO told a story like *that* before sharing big internal news with the staff, they'll have their audience warmed up and ready to say, "Yes! Let's do it!"

A story is like a fantastical drug for your brain. It takes us on a magic carpet ride as the storyteller moves through places that you may never visit in this reality, but for a moment, that story can transport you there. You literally feel more empathy, hope, determination, and commitment for change to occur. All from *that* story.

I challenge you, the next time you watch another presenter stand up and open with facts and figures, notice your own reaction. Are you excited and tuned in by that graph or market-share percentage? Or do you wish something more interesting was happening?

THE STORYTELLER'S POWER AND OBLIGATION

I want to re-share one of my favorite Steve Jobs' quotes:

*"The most powerful person in the world is the storyteller.
The storyteller sets the values, mission, and agenda for
an entire generation that is yet to come."*

Jobs was considered one of the most powerful business storytellers in modern history. His ability to pull his audience onto that magic carpet and take them on an emotional ride helped him build an empire that still stands as one of the most successful companies ever built, even after his premature passing. Apple's commercials were an extension of his storytelling moxie and their messaging of *their why* is what took them to the top. People were being introduced to the power of new technology like iTunes, the iPad, and iPhone through his storytelling abilities of demonstrating, and even constructing, the future. His stories aimed to awaken our emotions with the excitement of embracing a world we'd not experienced before. Jobs knew that sharing the vision through a story with real, relatable characters experiencing amazing new opportunities with the Apple brand would emotionally lock us into the buy-in. Those "characters" were you. No graph or pie chart did that in thirty seconds. His stories did.

> *The Storyteller's carefully chosen words, sounds, images, and story arc shape the Storyteller's Mind Movie.*

Our modern society has a short attention span. TikTok and Snapchat are conditioning our awareness and powers of observation—so as a presenter, you cannot risk boring your audience. (Not for one second. Do *not* bore them or you are scrolled over!) This book is going to show you how to use the power of storytelling skills to captivate because that is your obligation as the speaker. Share, enlighten, connect, and do it quickly. Get emotional images into your listeners' minds so that they *can't help* but see your vision with you.

CHAPTER FOUR

FINDING YOUR STORYTELLER'S MIND MOVIE

"So, how did you get into your line of work?"

For many people, this is a difficult question to answer. How do you feel when you answer it? Do you scramble to try and tell your own Story Fruition? Do you find your story entertaining and concise? Do you have several versions of your story to tell depending on your audience?

If you do, bravo! Keep up the great work building your own Story Library. But if you don't have a well-crafted response to that question and many other questions you'll get, then keep reading. We've got you.

Your story is as interesting—or uninteresting—as you make it. Personally, I want to be someone who shares stories that elevate the whole. I've finally realized that as I walk this planet for eight or nine decades (hopefully!), that I've got wisdom to share. My stories are like fine wine – they keep getting better with age.

Since your own Story Fruition is one of the most *important* and *valuable* stories that you can share as you grow your business, make sure you've got it down. This story is likely to also be told by your staff because your idea has a history attached to it. Prospects are going to want context; they are going to want to understand how you got to this brilliant idea that is likely to make a lot of money and success. Have this really well-crafted-and-entertaining story in your tool kit.

WHAT TO PUT IN YOUR OWN STORY FRUITION

Crafting the *full* version of your journey needs delicate thinking. It is not necessary to bog your listeners down with meticulous linear timeline events. For example, we don't need to know every apartment you rented before you finally bought the dream home. That may seem important to you, but a third party simply wants the highlights and the *Aha! Moment* that brought you to today. This is why story coaching helps because a coach has no preconceived notions about you and can provide you with clarity about when things are working, and when they might be meandering or confusing.

STORY-MINING YOUR LIFE

When did your career journey really start? How old were you? It may have been earlier than you think. I have many clients who have gone back and found key moments in their childhood that indicated their direction for their lives later on.

> *"I was ten years old, and my mother loved to drink Lipton iced tea in the summer. One day I thought, 'What if I made individual serving sizes for her?' So, I took out some small plastic sandwich bags and put one scoop of powered tea into them. I could smell the lemon as the powder wafted up into my nose when the spoon went into the jar. I then put the individual bags onto a pretty, silver tea tray and presented them to my mother. She was so touched by my thoughtfulness and my innovative mind. Who knew that individual servings would be so huge today? Too bad I didn't patent that idea then!"*
> *—KB, CEO, Digital Marketing Technology*

When was that first moment for you? That *key moment* when you realized that you needed to expand your horizons toward the idea you have brewing now? These *Aha! Moments* are exciting because they come from unexpected places. They're organic, seemingly coming from a place of inspiration beyond what we are aware of. There you were, just plodding along, when BOOM, an inciting event happens, you are then sent on a journey. You're at the right time in the right place—and suddenly you're part of a problem—but you instantly *know* the solution with *this* idea. You're forever changed by this moment.

Those are the moments that can be woven into your own Story Fruition (also known as an Origin Story.) The reason KB's story at ten is significant is because she is a serial entrepreneur and has been most of her life. Her mind just instantly and effortlessly sees the bigger picture and how to execute it. Most people buy into the linear living idea that you first: go to school, graduate, and then get a job that pays your salary, 401k, and your health insurance. If you are in government work, then your pension too. This is steady and predictable. Nothing wrong with it, and I've played that role and ridden those tracks in the first fifty years of my life. It's comfortable to some degree.

But to an entrepreneur, that is the equivalent of being put into a box without windows. KB did the "box" job in her early twenties at a major apparel company—and did well—but her creativity couldn't be satisfied within their corporate restraints. She wanted more and life heard her. Here's one of KB's stories that we crafted as part of her own Story Fruition. Watch how we playfully call her corporate employer, "The Box" and it's a vivid character in her story.

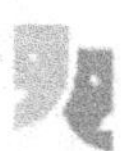

THE BOX

"I'm twenty-three, living in the Pacific Northwest, the place I've grown up and been for most of my life. The evergreen trees, snowcapped mountains, and bodies of water that decorate this part of the country make it truly one of the most picturesque areas of the United States. And like most people entering adulthood, I've sipped from the Kool-Aid and I know that everyone is supposed to go to a "real job" and get paid every two weeks, create a 401K, have health benefits, bond with your team, and output the product that The Box wants you to do. Seeing the great outdoors of my area becomes limited because the majority of my time is spent in The Box.

I worked for a major sporting manufacturer on the apparel side, and actually was clueless that the shoe side was where all the brand's notoriety was happening. For me, printing t-shirts that show the mid-drift, because this was the 1980s after all—mid-drifts and leg warmers were the rage, and I had my hands on the hot-off-the-printing-press status.

It was a good "job," and I loved my boss, Julie. She was one of the only female executives and her career was rising in her mid-thirties. She taught me to have a cool head when the situation was hot. She genuinely cared about her team. She made my work feel satisfying even though, deep down, I was stuck in The Box.

The Box led me into many cool opportunities, and I will always appreciate those times as my "launching pad." One of the great events was the trade show that was held twice a year. Textile companies from all over the country would spend big bucks to expose their t-shirts, threads, buttons, no-flake glitter technologies to The Box because landing us as an account could set your life. I knew almost everyone—and my mid-twenties peppy personality—made me popular, but I was also taken seriously for my knowledge of apparel.

The vendors, however, couldn't stand the man managing the show. He was rude, unorganized, and a pain to work with. So, one day, one of the owners of the trade show approached me. "KB, we'd like you to run this show for us. You can *have* the business. We will train you, of course, but we know that you can make this bigger and better." And a handshake later, I'm now the *owner*. My Inner Entrepreneur did not question it. It leapt out of The Box like a lioness kitten ready to play in the open wild.

The next day, I walked into Julie's office. She looked up at me and took this proposal I'd written (completely going off business instincts) and I said, "Julie, I quit and—you're going to hire me," with an enthusiastic grin on my face. She read the doc and replied, "You're not asking for enough money. Fix that and then we'll talk."

> Again, my Inner Entrepreneur didn't stop and chatter that "You can't do this! You're an imposter!" Nope. Didn't listen to one word. Instead, I put my head down, wrote out a strategy and business plan for the trade show and how The Box would fit into it dominantly, bravely increased my asking price, and....closed the deal.
>
> I ran that trade show for fifteen years."
>
> **KB, CEO, Digital Marketing**
>
> **Vancouver, WA**

In this story, we limit the characters to keep it easy to follow. We have KB, The Box, Julie, and three other "chorus" players running the tradeshows. That's all we need to make her Storyteller's Mind Movie launch and suspend interest for the listeners.

Now let's look at another situation where a story was not shared but stayed on the data train tracks. I witnessed this firsthand and affirmed that my work in this field would matter. Many leaders hate public speaking—but it's part of their game, and they flail around *faking it, until they make it, hopefully.*

DOCTOR DATA'S SWING AND A MISS

It's a sunny summer day in Bellevue, Washington. I'm standing in a bustling hotel conference room with 250 angel investors grabbing boxed sandwiches, sodas, iced water, and for some, decadent cookies wrapped in crunchy cellophane, just so that the whole room knows you're breaking your diet. They are here today to listen to the next big idea, their modern-day gold rush.

The stakes are high for the ten presenters. They have invested almost $20,000 to play in this five-city Pacific Northwest city tour and know that—after they present—they will be grilled by a litany of questions; smart, hard-hitting questions that an investor *must* know before they write that check. They are accredited, so if you land this meeting, your bank account grows, and your idea comes closer to its own fruition. This day matters.

I notice one presenter in the back of the room. He's hard to miss because he's the size of a Kodiak bear. He's wearing a silver-grey jacket and his badge says: Speaker. I look him up in the company booklet and see he's the CEO of a life science company and they are reducing tumors in ovarian cancer patients. *Wow. That's powerful and noble work. He is saving the lives of millions of women. I cannot wait to hear how he is doing that.*

I walk over and introduce myself and wish him luck. He smiles and says "Um...thank you. Uh....what do you do?"

Now I can tell that this man, this medical maverick, doesn't want to be in this room. He would much rather be in the lab looking at petri dishes and solving important and complex problems rather than hustling for funding. But now he has been pulled into this role and it's a part of the job.

"I'm a public speaking coach," I answer. His face goes pale, and he says, "Well, you're going to hate what I'm about to do! Will you excuse me?" and he dashed off. If he'd been Wyle E. Coyote, there would've been smoke puffs behind him he left so quickly. Public speaking was not his cup of ACME tea.

Speakers come on and off the stage, taking the spotlight, some sweating through it. Then it's the doctor's turn. The host does a terrific job of introducing him to the room. People in the audience have read his company bio. We are excited to hear him speak. The Kodiak approaches the stage, sheepishly. I could feel his dread for the next eight minutes. His mic goes on and he re-introduces himself. *Why is he doing that? We just heard from the host...?*

As I'm enjoying my boxed lunch sandwich, the doctor illuminates the screen with a giant picture of a lab rat with a tumor the size of a *baby's head* on its thigh and two huge graphs in reverse type behind it. Very scientific graphs with tons of decimal points and positive/negatives signs. *I'm not that smart. I don't understand what I'm reading.* The photo is shocking to the non-science folk in the room. I burp up my sandwich a bit.

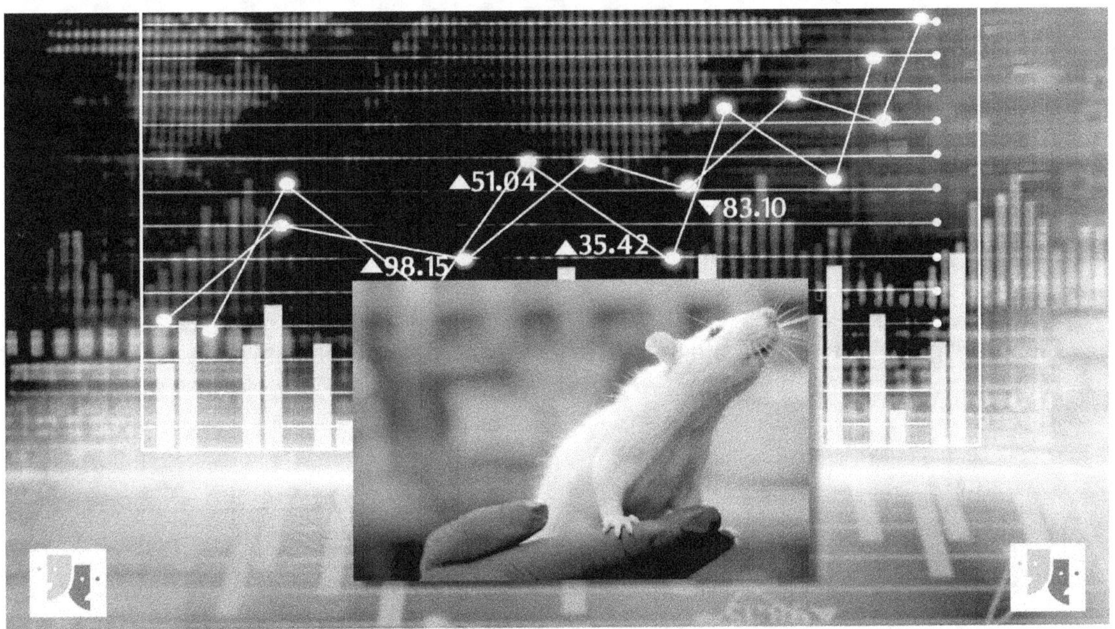

I'M OUT OF ACTIVE LISTENING TO THIS STORY DUE TO THE GRAPHIC.

His graphic image repels me. His too-in-the-lab-weeds-graph-too-soon took me *out of active listening. Literally, my brain is causing cortisol and adrenaline to increase and that causes discomfort.* He is epically failing to keep my attention by his own decision to show me something abrasive right out of the gate! And based on the wiggling in the room, I'm clearly not alone. There were a lot of half-eaten sandwiches thrown out that day.

This is an expensive swing and a miss.

SPEAK TO THE WHOLE ROOM, NOT JUST THE SCIENTISTS

As a scientist, Dr. Data lives, breathes, and constantly thinks about how he is going to heal women from the horrible condition that ovarian cancer is. This is literally about *life* and *death*. How can a graph humanize this truth? So, we must ask.... Who in his *own* life suffered at the hands of this disease, so much so—that it affected his drive to say, "I need to dedicate my life to solving this serious problem!"

Was it a family member? A friend? A neighbor? Or just a patient that he had met, looked into her eyes, and saw the fear and uncertainty of what the future suddenly could-or couldn't hold?

Tell *that* kind of story. Hook the audience. Open our hearts, connect us with our own humanity. Then show us the data to back up the severity. And now that pie chart has human connected *meaning*.

> *Your story puts heart behind the chart.*

If we were going to try this again, but instead of starting with the data and the unfortunate image of Tumor Rat...how would that experience look? Let's try this.

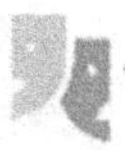

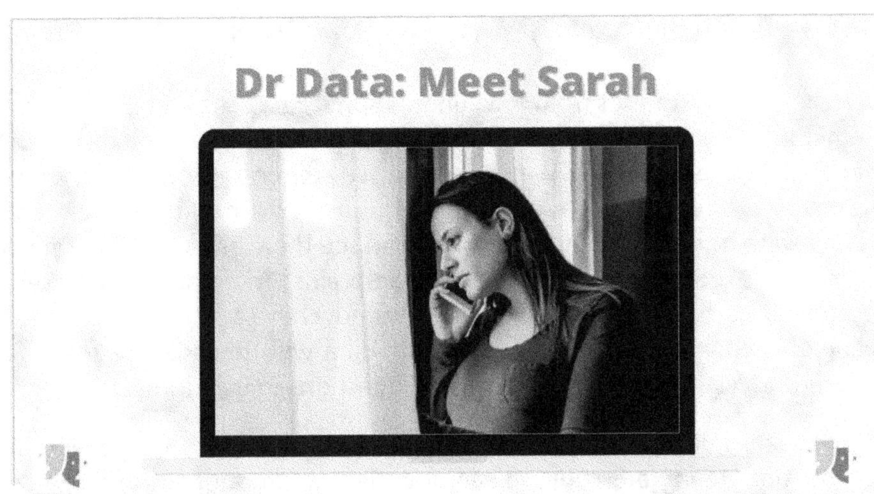

Meet Sarah. She's forty-two years old and has two tween kids, who both love soccer, and Sarah has to leave to go and pick them up from practice. She's on the phone, staring blankly out the bay window into their cul-de-sac, listening to her doctor give her some very disturbing news.

"Sarah… You've got Stage Two ovarian cancer, and we have some decisions to make," he says somberly. "You are one of the 22,000 cases that will be diagnosed this year. And we need to discuss the options that are going to work best for your situation."

Sarah sucks in her breath, but no air seems to want to come in as she listens.

"We will need to immediately increase the medications, and some will make you feel a little off your game. Woozy sometimes. And then we'll have to look at chemo...and possibly radiation....the next six months are going to be challenging..."

Sarah looks over at the Christmas tree. She sees some pine needles on the beige carpet. Normally that would irritate her, and she'd go vacuum them up...but right now...she just wants to smell that pine...cherish its aroma.

Will I be here for the next holiday? she asks herself.

Sarah is terrified.

The good news is that there is hope. Our company XYZ pharmaceutical has been diligently working on this problem, and we've seen groundbreaking results on the reduction of tumors like these in women like Sarah.

This year, of the 20,000 new cases of ovarian cancer diagnosed, there will be 12,000 ovarian cancer deaths in the United States. But at XYZ Labs, we're changing that problematic statistic.

Then, Dr. Data shows the lab rat and graphs!

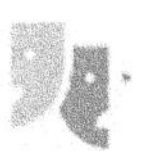

OPEN WITH A STORY TO HOOK YOUR AUDIENCE

What happens here? Dr. Data goes from cold, unemotional data stats and graphs that are barely nudging our minds to pay attention....to a *real story* of a *real person* that many of us, if not all of us, can see and relate to emotionally. We're hooked. We are rooting for Dr. Data to wear a cape and save the day. And, because he is a scientist, the business, math, and science *are* still there in his presentation so that the logical investor minds can see them and make informed decisions. But now, their hearts are overpowering their limbic brains. The rest of his presentation can now be the science/math of the business because we now have a foundational emotional-oxytocin-induced connection. The story infuses all the data with impact as a result. This keeps listeners engaged, which increases interaction and questions to be addressed.

This approach still delivers what the investors are looking for: problem, solution, addressable market, traction, team, etc., but we can now tie it in emotionally and remember it far longer than the opening graph. As Dr. Dahlstrom explains in his writings on narrative and the scientific community:

> *"Although storytelling often has negative connotations within science, narrative formats of communication should not be disregarded when communicating science to nonexpert audiences. Narratives offer increased comprehension, interest, and engagement. Nonexperts get most of their science from mass media content, which is itself already biased toward narrative formats. Narratives are also intrinsically persuasive, which offers science communicators tactics for persuading otherwise resistant audiences."*
> —Michael F. Dahlstrom, PhD, Iowa State University

BRINGING LIFE TO THE DATA AND NUMBERS

Let's explore the power of graphs and charts for presentations because they are vital, and they all hold stories. How you tell it is key. You can simply read the numbers and interpret the data back to the audience, or you can find a story that captivates your audience and makes them relate to the numbers. Dr. Chip Heath, a Stanford professor in Organization Behavior, found that 63 percent of people could remember stories they were told versus only 5 percent remembering a statistic or graph. So how can we balance those two different types of storytelling?

LOOKING FOR THE DATA'S STORY

One time, I was in a meeting listening to a founder explain his business's growth. He flashed a graph that exhibited some impressive sales for his merchant-payment system. Sales were chugging along beautifully. Then May of 2020 hit, and it plummets. He points to a dramatic dip in the graph and says, "See that? That's the pandemic!"

That's short and sweet—but we need more. "That's the pandemic," just opens everyone in the room to figure out what he means. And as the audience individually wonders, *"Is that number the amount of PPE we needed, even before we heard that term before?"*

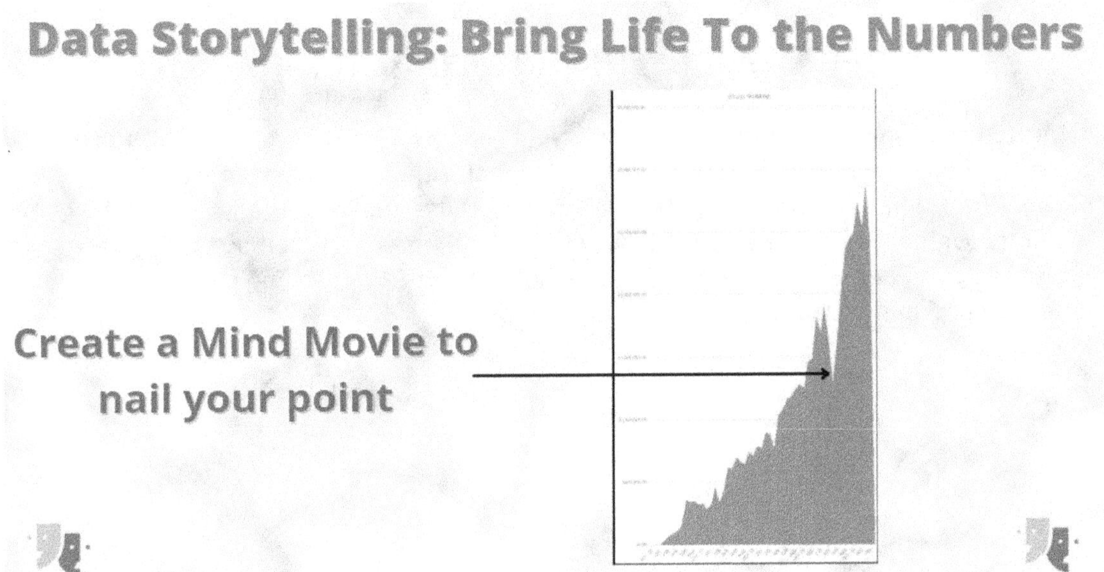

EXPAND ON THE JUICY DETAILS.

Let's play to see how we can pull out a story rich with images to create a Mind Movie. An example could be mining experiences from our own collective lives. Try expanding on that time to engage our memories and invoke *images* and *emotions.*

"See here? Electronic sales were going great. My restaurant clients were flourishing. My auto mechanics couldn't be happier. Business was robust and all were chugging along. Then the world seemed to stop. We were suddenly living in a 3D world, sequestered into a 2D Zoom reality. We were told to:

'Stay home! Wash your hands! Wash your groceries! Wear gloves! Wear a mask! We think!'

The pandemic-surreal world was collectively holding its breath for those who couldn't breathe. It was chaotic and scary. *It was global pandemonium.*

But humans are resilient.

Slowly and steadily, we learned how to adapt to *the new normal*; we found safe ways to interact with one another again. We started buying and selling again, and electronic media was our savior.

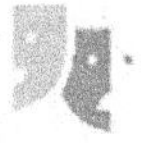

And my company was there to help it happen. We worked closely, helping them create contact-less payment methods, and like a QR code, we became heroes. And I can't be prouder of my team for responding as quickly as they did."

DATA, MEET STORY. STORY, MEET DATA

As I watch so many entrepreneurs and company leaders continue to open with facts and figures, without any regard for the brain's emotional experience, I am convinced this must change. The traditional model needs to change because the world, now completely connected through online experiences, allows us to see an idea and then instantly research it. The presentation deck is not the be-all-and-end-all of facts. We can find stories and will find stories to back up the claim.

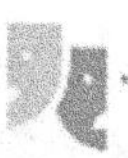

CHAPTER FIVE

FINDING YOUR STORIES OF TRANSFORMATION

How do you craft a story that is well structured and achieves the results you are seeking? How do you keep the focus of the listeners' attention as you paint the Storyteller's Mind Movie? It's simple: Follow the Story Arc.

Joseph Campbell published *The Hero with A Thousand Faces* in 1949, and with it he gave a formulaic structure that many artists followed, including George Lucas for *Star Wars*. In fact, Disney/Pixar utilize this journey in all of their stories, as it clearly sets up the story's hero and their transformation. I teach this in my workshops and use it all the time when composing my own stories for stage. At my improv theater, all of the ensemble has been trained to follow this formula as we make up stories on-the-fly.

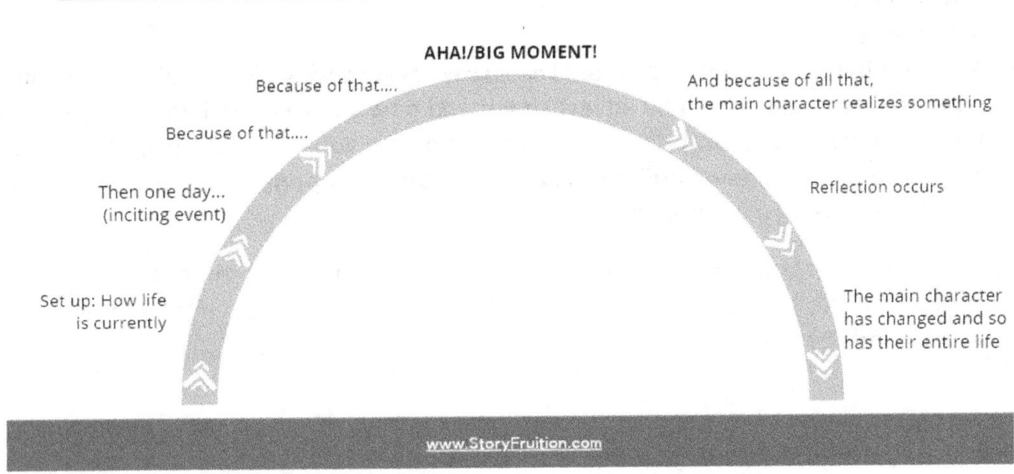

PROCESS ONE: STORY MINING

We start with an *Aha!* Moment. One of my mentors, Matthew Dicks, in his book, *Storyworthy*, (a must read for all personal-life storytellers) says that our stories center around five seconds of time. A moment after a series of events where you come to realize something that you had not seen or understood before. You changed in that one *Aha!* Moment. We are loaded with these moments, both personally and professionally, because we are the same person on a journey—in a variety of different circumstances.

PROMPT THE STORY OUT OF YOU

As you read these prompts, get a notebook or grab your accompanying *The Storyteller's Mind Movie Journal*, and allow the experience that pops into your mind. That's a story waiting to be developed. Trust it. Some stories are going to flow effortlessly out of you, and some will stay back and come out when they are ready to be told, but they are both brewing. What we are looking for are the *Aha!* Moments that changed you.

Jot down in a notebook what comes to mind. Just list a person, or the title of an event you recall. You may only have one idea, but for some of these you may have a few people or situations that jump out. I encourage you to write them all down. This list is for your eyes, so don't be shy.

- **Best Boss**
- **Worst Boss**
- **Best Customer**
- **Worst Customer**
- **First Job**
- **Last Job**
- **Jobs I loved**
- **Jobs I hated**
- **Moment in childhood that pointed me to my career today** (Get creative. Did you rock your first lemonade stand by advertising it and now you're a marketer? Or perform as the top seller for the wrapping paper drive and now you're in enterprise level sales?)
- **The moment you knew you had to start your own company** (if you have or are thinking about starting a company).

Next, choose one of the prompts that is prodding you inside to come out to play. Set a timer for five minutes and then just let go. Write without stopping. No editing. When time is up, then stop and see what bubbled up.

Good work! As you keep reading, we will start crafting these stories and moving them towards your Storyteller's Mind Movie!

STORY FRUITION EXAMPLES FOR FOUNDERS

As mentioned earlier, there are three kinds of entrepreneurs and inventors:

1. Those who fix something that is broken.

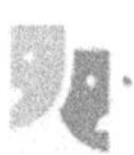

2. Those who expand something that already exists and is ready for the next level.
3. Those who create something unique.

Which one are you?

All of these have strong stories paired with real problems—as well as the solutions—waiting for you to uncover in your narrative. I've pitched hundreds of founders for Founders Live Seattle and the Seattle University's Business School competition, and I've heard so many remarkable ideas of how people are going to change the world. Here are a few.

1. FIXING SOMETHING THAT IS BROKEN

***Go Love Yourself Box*, Sharon Podobnik-Peterson, CEO**
Competitor in Founders Live Seattle

One of my favorite Story Fruitions is from a spunky, smart CEO, Sharon Podobnik-Peterson, whom I connected with the second we met when she arrived to compete in Seattle's Founders Live. The CEO of Founders Live, my friend, Nick Hughes, gathers five entrepreneurs who share how they are going to change the world....in just ninety-nine seconds. That's right, one minute and thirty-nine seconds. The audience then votes for the best pitch, and they win prizes and media accolades. I'm the Seattle pitch coach for Nick and I help the founders find their story that highlights the problem, and then position their company as the hero with the problem-solving solution. **In those precious ninety-nine seconds we find the story, go-to market, addressable market, traction/accolades, team, and the ASK all in that time frame.** It's a challenge, but many Founders Live contestants have gone on to use their Founders Live Pitch to attract millions of dollars from investors. Nick does this every month all over the globe in over sixty markets and the crowd that comes is filled with entrepreneurs, investors, advisors, and talent looking for the next big idea. The energy of Founders Live is one of support and celebration, that these founders' dreams have legs and the courage to run with it.

GO LOVE YOURSELF

It's Tuesday before the Thursday Founders Live show and there is one founder I still haven't heard from, so I reach out and she quickly responds with an appointment an hour later. This energetic woman with her beautiful smile is a driven woman who works well under pressure.

She shares she had been a schoolteacher ten years before, so she was constantly under the gun of deadlines and was used to this kind of pressure. She had created an impressive group of women who sought community to help them with their mental anxiety.

Go Love Yourself Box is a monthly subscription of mental health tools for women to study with other like-minded women. (Think Stitch Fix meets Book Club.) Your box arrives and it's filled with the book of the month, herbal teas, scented candles, etc., all designed to help the receiver enjoy the personal and professional growth process, learn how to strike a work/life balance—and realize that we women don't have to carry the whole world on our shoulders. That our natural instinct is to do it all, and to do it all perfectly: Work, cook, clean, raise the kids, and that's just not true. No one wrote that law, it's been handed down to us through our cultural constructs—and Sharon knew things had to change.

I asked Sharon, "So, what do you do?" She paused. "What do I do?" and then, mechanically, said, "I work with female CEOs and executives and help them provide better leadership...through...understanding.... Oh, I *hate* that question!"

"That's probably asked a lot, isn't it?"

"Yes, and I hate how I can't handle it."

"Okay," I coached. "What's your story? How did you come up with this idea? It's unique..."

And then she let go. She dropped all of her tension and traveled back in time to when she was on the brink of a nervous breakdown in her early thirties. Her own story was the impetus to her creating this company (which is the case for most CEOs/founders). She quit her position as Director of Academics and followed her instincts to make the *Go Love Yourself Box*, something that could change the world.

Sharon returned fifteen hours later with her slides and story ready to go. Her deck was clean, easy to follow, and her story was vulnerable, full circle and she wove in all the investor elements brilliantly.

She opened her ninety-nine seconds with an image of a woman on her bed in her pajamas, crying with her laptop on her lap.

Meet Sharon. She's thirty-two years old and she's had it. She's on this unending hamster wheel of hell. She pops Prozac in the morning and Ambien at night just to get through the day. She's up long before the sun rises and doesn't notice when the sun has set. As she scrolls through the pages of Facebook, she thinks, 'I wish I could do cool stuff like that, I wish.' Do you ever feel that way? Do you want to believe that life has more to offer than just the daily grind?

Sharon then shows images of the product and her business model; the community she's grown, and her traction being featured on *Good Morning America, HuffPo,* and *Oprah!* Then she closed with her ask.

"I'm Sharon, the founder of the Go Love Yourself Box, and I'm standing in front of you two years later, proof that this works. Sharon is calm, journaling with Earl grey each morning, and meditating with chamomile each night."

Sharon took 70 percent of the votes that night and went on to win the competition. Her vulnerable and true Story Fruition was a perfect beginning to highlight the problem. Her presentation then went on with very simple visuals and hardly any copy. We want the listeners

to be on her words and full attention; not bogged down by wordy or confusing graphs that can prevent the audience from actively listening.

2. EXPANDING UPON SOMETHING THAT EXISTS AND IS READY FOR THE NEXT LEVEL

***Easeenet*, Estate Planning, Erin McCune, Founder/CEO**
Portland, OR

I met Erin McCune, CEO of *Easeenet,* when I was invited to be a panelist for the Seattle Angel's Conference. The founder of the highly respected SAC, John Sechrest, invited fifty-six of his incubator companies to do a one-minute pitch that myself and two other angel investors would hear and provide feedback on. The person who leapt out of the crowd was Erin McCune. Her ability to fill sixty seconds with commanding images of what *Easeenet* offers and *why* she's doing it—and is already making money—impressed the panel. I then started working directly with her to finetune her storytelling for her marketing. Erin is one of the refreshing founders who love to learn and grow, which is so helpful when working on a client's storytelling skills.

According to Easeenet's research, the average amount of time to close out an estate when a will *is* in place—is a whopping *570 hours*. It's exhausting, depressing, and frustrating—all while you're grieving. Here's Erin's story and what started her on her entrepreneurial journey. Clearly the arduous and emotionally draining system needs fixing to help grieving people navigate a complicated system. This honest and vividly told story is great for podcasts and is in Erin's Story Library.

EASEENET'S STORY FRUITION (FULL VERSION)

I am twenty-four and my husband and I are playing hooky from work. We are on our way to lunch (and maybe a bit of day drinking) when we get a call from his brother saying he'd found my fifty-eight-year-old father-in-law (whom I called "Dad") unconscious in the garden! "An ambulance is on the way," his brother says in panic.

Dad had suffered an aneurysm, and if you're not familiar with the scale, a Grade One is a horrible headache, and a Grade Five is instant death. His is a Grade Four, and he is given a 20 percent chance of survival by the doctors.

Dad wakes up the next morning, in good spirits, but with less than a ten-second memory. I spend hours alone in his ICU hospital room while he repeats the same ten-second loop. He sits up, and says:

"I need to pee."

"No, Dad, you have a catheter in."

"No, I don't," he says defiantly.

"Yes, you do," I reply knowingly.

Then, whoosh, he throws open his blanket in all his male glory only to confirm that there is, in fact, a catheter in. Satisfied that he does, indeed, have a catheter in, he leans back in bed. Less than a minute later, he's sitting up again.

"Dad, what do you need?"

"I need to pee."

"No, Dad, you have a catheter in."

"No, I don't."

"Yes, you do!"

Then whoosh, off goes the blanket again. (I am seeing more than I have ever wanted to see of Dad). Again, and again. What seems hilarious when it happens three times over loses its humor by the three hundredth time, and the grief washes over me like a tsunami. After four hours, I tell the nurses, "I am exhausted and going to the bathroom." I feel like I am drowning, sobbing without sound in the austere ICU bathroom.

When I walk back into his room, there is a flurry of activity, with several nurses and a frightening number of large splatters of blood on the bed, the walls, even the ceiling. He has pulled out the stent in his brain in the few minutes I'd stepped away! That stent is meant to keep his brain from further damage after his surgery, but it is now even riskier to try and put back in.

Dad spent two weeks in ICU, two weeks in a brain injury clinic, and then required months of supervised recovery. He didn't know where he was or what year it was. And the problem was, he was the primary caretaker at the time for his eighty-eight-year-old mother, which meant that the full responsibility for Dad's life and Grandma's life were now on my husband and me.

Since Dad is only fifty-eight, little to no thought has been given to estate planning, and we have to wade through countless files and hours of paperwork trying to caretake things for Dad. Grandma has minimal motor skills and pretty advanced dementia; she cried when she tried to sign the paperwork for a special needs trust for Dad because she couldn't remember how to sign her name. She requires the full-time care that Dad had been providing, and my husband and I just aren't able to offer it to her.

We try to put Dad and Grandma in the same adult foster care home, but Dad keeps sneaking out the front door and getting lost a block or two away in the neighborhood. Tensions flare high with other family members accusing us of "warehousing" Dad when we move

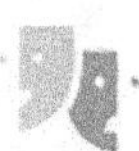

him to a memory care community. We are just doing the very best we can with the limited resources and knowledge we have. Our marriage and finances suffer. Hours of every week are spent searching for their files and accounts to help keep bills paid. We spend hours on hold, navigating phone trees, searching through files and boxes of mail, providing documentation, filling out forms.

We are walking through a blind snowstorm every time someone asks for the username and password. This is a *new* ring in Dante's Hell.

Unexpectedly taking care of someone's affairs is exhausting and daunting, even if you have access to all the information. Paying attorney's fees for power of attorney for both Dad *and* his mom is not an easy feat to achieve. And then you are still constantly proving your role because everyone needs identification and proof that you have power of attorney.

ERIN WEAVES DATA INTO HER STORY

When we have to take over for Dad and Grandma's assets, bills, and records, pretty much everything was offline. But today adds an entirely new set of challenges, because unless you take care of it ahead of time, many accounts are inaccessible or downright *invisible* to your next of kin. The average American now has over 200 logins connected to their email account, so dealing with countless logins and passwords seems like a war you can't win. Many people use automatic payments and paperless billing, so you no longer know exactly what bills there are or what needs to be paid. Horror stories of the electricity being turned off for nonpayment, and Grandpa's car getting towed away by the repo man because no one knew he still had a car payment.

When I had the idea for *Easeenet*, it was to simplify the Internet and make it easy to see— for you today, and your family tomorrow. Of course, I assumed that someone had to have already thought of this, in our 'there's an app for that' world, but no. No one had thought of it like I was seeing it.

Enter *Easeenet*: the easiest way to declutter, organize, and preserve your online life today, so it doesn't wreak havoc on your loved ones when you're no longer able to take care of your own affairs.

EASEENET SHORTER VERSION?

The first time I had to take over a relative's estate, I was twenty-four. My husband and I had played hooky for the day when we got a chilling phone call. His fifty-eight-year-old dad, whom I also called Dad, had suffered an aneurysm and was being rushed to the hospital. He was given a 20 percent chance of surviving his brain surgery. Fortunately, he survived, but he woke up the next morning with a ten-second memory.

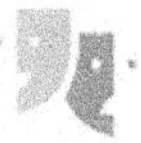

As if that wasn't enough, Dad was the sole caretaker for his eighty-eight-year-old mother who had late-stage dementia. Our lives changed in an instant. My husband and I had to take over everything for both Dad and Grandma— using the limited resources and knowledge available to us.

Unexpectedly taking care of someone's affairs is exhausting and daunting, even if you have access to all of the information. When we had to take over for Dad and Grandma, everything was offline, so today adds an entirely new set of challenges because unless you take care of it ahead of time, many accounts are inaccessible or downright invisible to your next of kin.

The average American now has over 200 logins connected to their email account, so dealing with countless logins and passwords seems like a war you can't win. Many people use automatic payments and paperless billing, so you no longer know exactly what bills there are or what needs to be paid. I've heard horror stories of the electricity being turned off for nonpayment, and Grandpa's car getting towed away by the repo man because no one knew he still had a car payment.

Easeenet simplifies the Internet and makes it easy to see— for you today, and your family tomorrow.

—Erin McCune, Founder/CEO, Easeenet
Portland, OR

3. ENTREPRENEURS CREATING SOMETHING NEW

Advocat.AI, Law Tech, Pradnya Desh, Founder/CEO
Bellevue, WA

I met the CEO of Advocat.AI, Pradnya Desh, at Founders Live Seattle. Like many founders before her, she only had ninety-nine-seconds to show us how she'd change the world. She is an attorney and a former US diplomat, so public speaking is something she is quite comfortable with on a daily basis. She did, however, open her pitch by quoting facts and figures, which by now, you know I raised a flag. Pradnya had witnessed far too many times how expensive attorney fees are for clients because hours upon hours are billed for research that attorneys must do to build their cases, all on the client's dollar. Due to the massive, usually unplanned, expenses that arise, there can be emotionally and financially crippling consequences, like the loss of homes, the loss of custody of children, and bankruptcy. Pradnya was appalled that in a democratic society, where everyone has the right to good legal advice, exorbitant costs were preventing people from getting their fair time in the legal system. That's The Problem.

During my initial interview with her, I had seen her deck, and it was very smart and logical. She had all the facts and figures—but it lacked an emotional connection. I asked her, "Is there a particular client that comes to mind who really struck a chord with you and motivated you to start Advocat?"

And, without hesitation, Pradnya said, "Yes!" She then shared the highly emotional, first-hand experience she had with Emily and Jenn. It was a moving experience that transformed the way Pradnya saw her job and inspired her to change a system that was broken. So, Pradnya Desh founded Advocat.AI.

HERE'S THE FOUNDERS LIVE SEATTLE NINETY-NINE-SECOND PITCH

Meet Emily. She is a former army sergeant who served in Afghanistan. She and her best friend, Jenn, also an army sergeant, saved up their money so that they could start an organic cosmetics company when they left the army. And that's when I met them. They had purchased supplies and created some awesome colors. They had a dream to start their own cosmetic company.

They came to my law firm needing legal employment and regulatory advice. We quoted them the time we'd need, and it would be $4000 for the set up and employment advice, and another $20,000 for the regulatory advice. They said yes to the $4000 but skipped the regulatory advice because it was too expensive. **That is when I felt it in the pit of my stomach**, because you can't just skip regulatory advice. They didn't have the extra $20,000.

They released their product to the market—and four months later, the FDA shut them down. Emily and Jenn, who had dreamed of a new life and had served their country, had their dreams shattered because legal services are too expensive!

This happens all the time to moms and dads who need to keep custody of their kids; people who need to keep custody of their houses—So. Much. Heartbreak. And I, as a lawyer, couldn't take it anymore. So, I pulled together a team of artificial intelligence experts and founded Advocat.AI—and now look at what we can do!

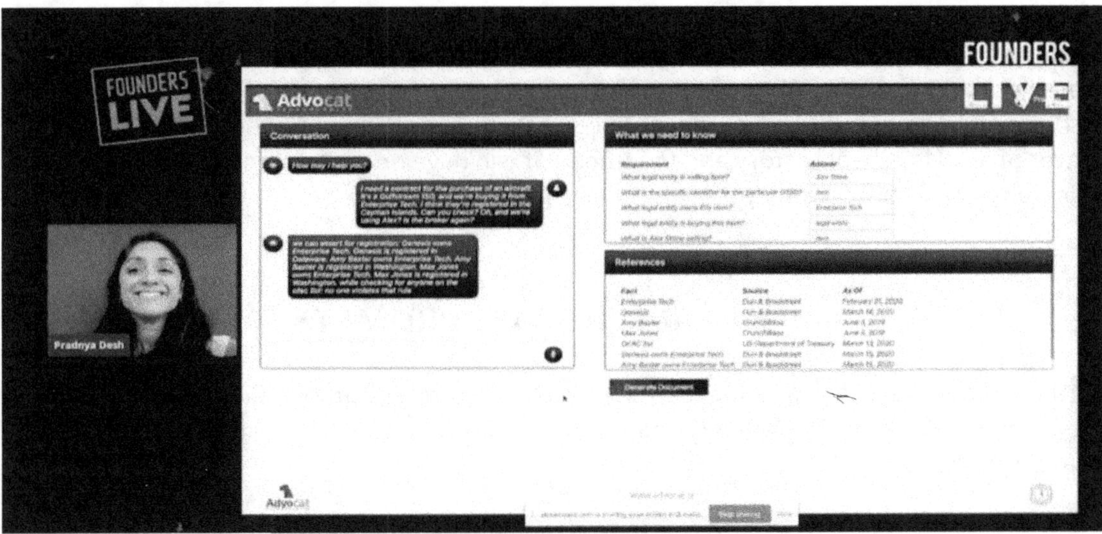

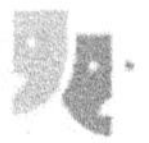

This is Advocat's A.I. and if Emily were to come to me today, I could tell Advocat what I need. It would then ask me questions and I would instantly receive cases, templates, and well-researched documents, saving me hours of attorney time and saving thousands of dollars for the client. We are revolutionizing law!

This is a powerful and personal Story Fruition built around Pradnya's *Aha!* Moment with Jenn and Emily that Pradnya continues to use for her capital fundraising. And she's repeatedly winning competitions with this pitch and other story infused versions. Pradnya quickly learned the power of storytelling in her fundraising. She has pitched one-minute, five-minute, ten-minute, and one-to-one meetings to close over $2.3M in funding. Pradnya learned that the power of storytelling helped the investor *see* and *feel* the vision with her.

> *"When you're on your start-up journey, all you have is this vision,*
> *and it's the stories that help you to share the vision."*
> —Pradnya Desh, Founder/CEO, Advocat.AI

STORY PROMPTS BY LIFE CHAPTERS

As you move through your life, you are picking up chapters that are filled with thousands of "Aha! Moments," and you just need to identify which ones want to come out. I often get challenged by clients when we start our private coaching sessions, that they lack stories of interest, and that is only true because they haven't learned *how* to tell their stories yet. Story prompts can uncover memories rapidly—and then learning how to craft the story scene-by-scene is how the Mind Movie is born.

This is a quick list of **some** "Life Chapters" that we enter by decades that are loaded with stories that can be universal and relatable to 'where you are at in life.' And with each one, we have a clear state of mind—or *where* we are mentally and spiritually in life. Take your time and jot down moments that resonate as they bubble up in your story prompt notebook or the accompanying journal. We will then look at how you can take these stories and tie them into a business use case story. You may drum up a childhood memory story that could be used in a company town hall setting, or any public-speaking opportunity. Never underestimate the power of any Life Chapter story and the impact it can have on your listeners' buy in. Personal vulnerability and transparency are what make great leaders.

LIFE CHAPTER STORY PROMPTS

Let's play inside decades and life stages with the following prompts. Circle the decade you are in, and the ones you've already completed. And highlight the playful prompts that spark your memories.

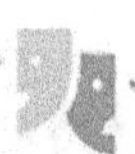

Tweens/Teens: Loving toys; embarrassed about your "little kid toys" as you move to teens; hormones; fear or curiosity of sexuality; gender identity; family dynamic influences; school graduations; extra-curricular activities; GPAs matter (or don't); fashion confusion; popular kids vs "nerds" vs bullies. Riding the school bus or walking to school; grandparents' wisdom while you still have access to it.

Twenties: Finding your identity. Graduating college and/or finding a job; your first time living on your own; exploring the job market to find the perfect fit. Will your actual degree matter? Learning that you may not care, and will rather find something cool that you believe in. *Puppy Adult Dating (young adults out in the wild)* and learning to swipe right only when you mean it; getting engaged; not getting engaged; working to climb the ladder, but still a powerless plebe; renting apartments and learning personal finance; flying from the nest; not flying from the nest; having babies and spouses; not having babies and spouses.

Thirties: Career growth; finding your groove; proving yourself personally and professionally; marriage and family building accelerating; or comparing yourself to not having a family yet; money growth; home buying; upgrading cars; new manager or finding your place more solidly in your career; building your start-up; getting your ego kicked by the investor community and learning to pivot; struggling to make ends meet; or finally getting the white picket fence and a dog. If you are a parent, navigating the balance of work/home life balance.

Forties: Becoming a "Rising Star" at work because you never say "No"; stagnant at work; keeping up with the Jones' and knowing you make more than they do; or you make less than they do and are sick of their bragging; questioning why that really even matters? Kids are in middle school, so there's parenting pressure to keep up with academics: soccer games, PTA meetings, and HOA dues; country clubs; no country club; vacations; saving for college or getting kids ready for sports scholarships; cocktail parties and conversations of Who's Who; addiction taking over your life; debt or prosperity? Challenges with diet/health issues may be kicking in; divorce? "Mid-life course corrections"; mid-life crises; learning to online date again—but feeling like a Puppy Adult, but older and not as spry and much more opinionated; learning to reinvent yourself and respect your own resilience.

Fifties: Climb the corporate ladder or jumped off to start your own business because your new boss rocks (that's you); mentoring younger rising talent to take the torch; managing a Merger & Acquisition; being comfortable in your career status; changing your career. Personal front: hating online dating; that person you've pined for since your twenties—you look them up on Facebook; friends trying to set you up; career thriving but mental health issues could be creeping in from exhaustion; mid-life assessment of what's been attained and what is far off; divorce or remarriage and starting fresh; that person you've pined for since your twenties—you message. Your older kids failing to launch; or kids are top of their game and your sense of parental pride; Botox and Pilates to ward off aging. Feeling young; feeling old. Looking at retirement and wondering how you'll do it? Looking at retirement and ready to roll; your aging parents are becoming a concern and you are the Adult Child parenting your kids and now your parents (and you can't tell who has grumpier fits); your parents need you more than ever; now living with you? Reinvention of your personal brand; AARP wants to be your friend and not sure how you feel about it

Sixties: You're getting ready to retire; your favorite clients and colleagues that helped get you to where you are; Pensions? No pensions; retirement parties and the sentimentality of it all; choosing to go grey or keep it under cover; health issues may be more of a topic with either you or your classmates; early death of classmates and feeling your mortality; looking to finally retire and downsize or move to a warmer place; grand babies or no grand babies; loss of our younger bodies and faces; if you're single, it can feel lonely or it can feel quite liberating; many are on a "next-life-partner hunt"; Neptune Society has you on their mailing list.

Seventies: Only flat shoes in your closet; body feels achy; things are sagging more than they did, but you learn how to dress to cover them; or you let it all hang out; carefree attitude because you are in your fourth quarter of life and it's going to be your best one; appreciation for more depth from your life because you understand tomorrow is not a guarantee; spirituality may be intensifying; grand kids are your mark of legacy and highly valued; holidays and Sunday dinners matter more; driving is getting challenging; memory is starting to slip and that's scary; you develop new hobbies because time is ticking; golf, tennis, walking, and some biking are wonderful ways to stay fit; travel dreams are coming to life because again, now is the best time physically.

Eighties/Nineties/and above: Widow and widowers more prevalent; sense of purpose feels challenging; technology is for the kids; body aches, but mind still feels sharp, or mind is clearly duller; meds are for breakfast; senior care reality; plot shopping, burden on the kids; Grandparent Sage; appreciation of the now; you're the storyteller who preserves your family history.

Spark anything? What prompts spark memories and lessons?

You know the drill. Get out your journal or notebook and grab a pen. Or fire up your keyboard.

1. Set your timer for five minutes.
2. Choose one prompt and let it flow.
3. No editing. Just let it out.
4. Stop when the timer rings.

How does that story make you feel? Where are the nuggets of wisdom? Congratulations, you just added a story to your own Story Library!

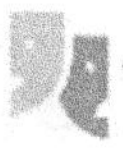

PROCESS ONE RECAP: STORY MINING

1. Your stories matter and when you share them, your leadership becomes inspiring and magnetic.
2. To stand out and increase your worth 50 percent more, master your communication skills.
3. Storytelling is an essential business skill. Invest in it.
4. The Storyteller has the power and the obligation to educate and entertain their listeners.
5. People are inspired by *why* you do what you do, so make sure your stories show that.
6. Your brain reacts differently with data and analytics vs when it processes a story.
7. Stories spark emotions and that is where decisions are made, so tell stories to balance out the data—and to transform you to an Emotionally Connected Leader!
8. Stories put heart into your chart!
9. Story-mine your experiences throughout your life, including childhood, to craft your own Story Fruition, which is one of the most important stories to tell.
10. To be a great storyteller, it takes work—and "the work" is so much fun! Enjoy the adventure.

PROCESS TWO
STORY CRAFTING

SETTING UP YOUR MIND MOVIE
SCENE BY SCENE

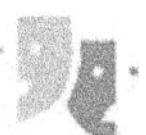

CHAPTER SIX

FOLLOWING A STORY ARC

Your Story of Transformation

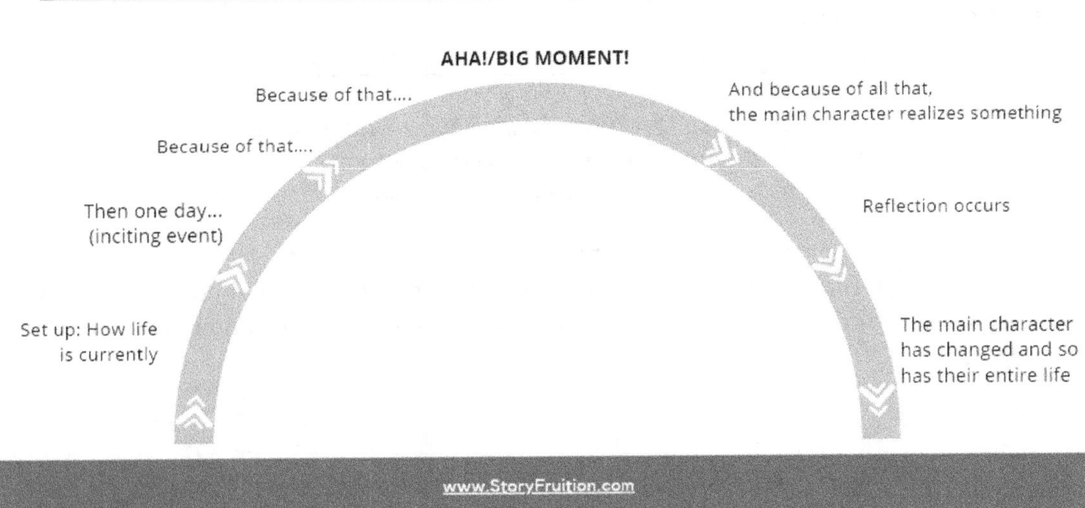

Congratulations, Storyteller-in-the-making—you've identified a few stories that *want* to bust out of you. You have emotions tied to it. You know the characters that were involved. Now we must clearly and concisely construct your story so that it glides the listener from first word to last word, so that it becomes an exciting and interesting journey you place the listeners on with you. It teaches a great life lesson and changes who you are as an evolving leader. So how do we begin it? How do we travel through it? And how do you end it to leave them gloriously delighted or moved to the action you seek? Let's now break it down, step-by-step.

> **START your story from the point *before* you realized there was a problem**

All stories are surrounding the *Aha! Moment*, but the start of the story is the most important part. The set up establishes the main character (you or your target market persona) and how life normally operates. Status quo existence, as I like to say. We learned earlier, Erin McCune was going to have lunch and enjoy some playful day drinking with her husband; Pradnya Desh

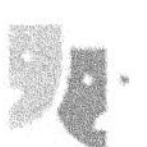

just wanted to help a client set up their company and live their dream. And Sharon Podobnik-Peters was on the brink of a meltdown.

But then one day... *something* suddenly happened that shook the foundation of the status quo—and from that, a series of actions and people show up that initiate the event. Conflict has entered the picture and then...

This happens...

Then that happens...

Until... BOOM! The light bulb moment! The Problem gets resolved, learned, realized. And then the protagonist (you or your target audience persona) changes, and your new world, the new normal, is established.

> *All of these lifetimes of experiences add up and then: You become who you are today.*
> *Your life is a real page turner*

Transformation requires that we lose something—we become willing (or fight against it) to let go of the world as we have known it up until this moment—and now must adjust into the new reality.

STAKES AND TRANSFORMATION MUST BE CLEAR

As you compose and craft your stories for your presentations, it's important that *The Problem* is where you reveal the stakes. In my own Story Fruition, the stakes of getting an income that brought me joy – and to be physically available for my daughter – were high.

Business stories show your why, so let's make them captivating.

If you're doing a target market persona story, then your character is experiencing emotions about the problem you are solving.

- Will they have good health or bad health?
- Will they make money or crash?
- Will they see the beauty life offers, or spiral downward and onto a hamster wheel of perpetual dissatisfaction?

You, or your company brand, then plays the role of the hero in the story of transformation. That means your story needs to have an array of emotions and stakes.

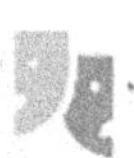

Here are some emotional ranges to guide you. Moving the story from one of the emotions on the left and to an opposite, more empowered emotion on the right is the goal for the end of your business story.

Emotional Words for Transformation

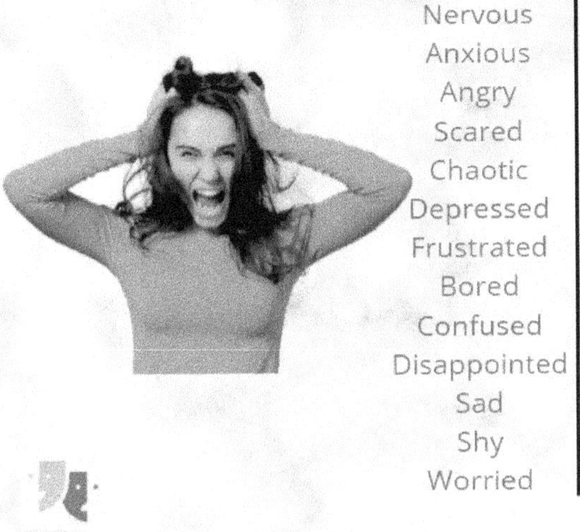
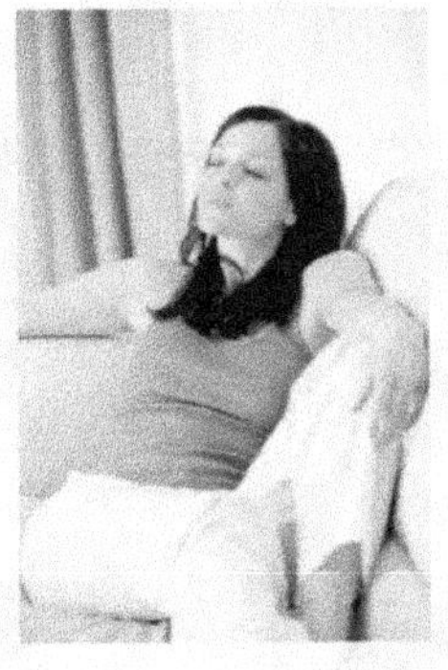

Nervous	Relaxed
Anxious	Carefree
Angry	Pleased
Scared	Laid-back
Chaotic	Calm
Depressed	Joyous
Frustrated	Relieved
Bored	Entertained
Confused	Clearheaded
Disappointed	Thrilled
Sad	Happy
Shy	Confident
Worried	Unconcerned

As you craft your story, the main character's life is plugging along, until the inciting event occurs, and then the list on the left may be your source of conflict and tension. As the story unfolds, and the Aha! Moment reveals itself, then the words on the right column may be your result. That's transformation and that makes your story more interesting and memorable, so always look for the transformation and paint your Mind Movie to reflect it.

CHAPTER SEVEN

C.R.O.W. IS NOT JUST FOR THE BIRDS

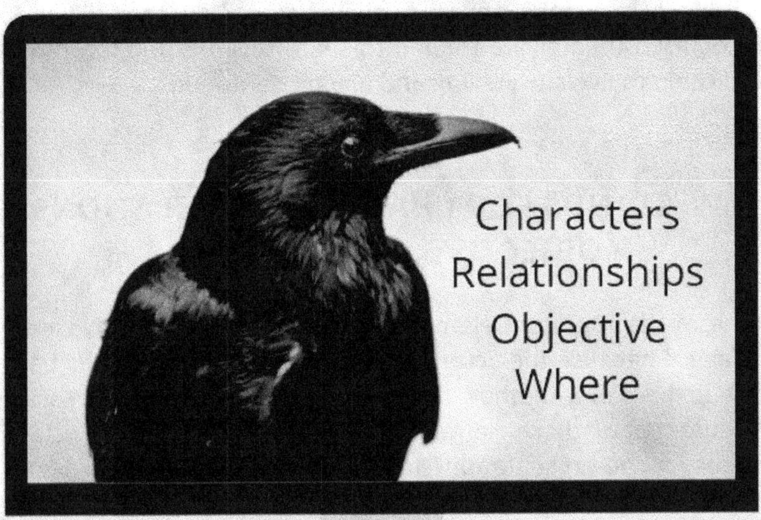

This is the most important part of learning storytelling structure and how to go from being an average storyteller to a brilliant Mind Movie Maker! I want you to put that bird in your mind and *hold onto it* with every story you start crafting for your personal or professional Story Library. Whether it's a quick, thirty-second pitch story, your company's Story Fruition, or a customer success story that may take a minute and a half to tell, the exciting, yet challenging, part of any story is *starting* it. This is where everything gets established for your listeners. You are going to introduce yourself, other characters, and take us on your adventure, that leads to a conclusion. When you are clear, the story works beautifully as your Mind Movie takes on a life of its own in our imaginations. But when you are vague and bland, so is your Mind Movie. And your audience goes limp. We don't want them bored, so how do we prevent that? *Read on, my wise grasshopper.*

THERE ARE SO MANY DOORS YOU CAN OPEN
TO START THE JOURNEY

Sometimes it makes sense to start really close to the moment you had the realization. Sometimes the journey took a little longer, so you'll need to do some advanced time-travelling techniques, but the most important thing to remember is to keep the story vivid and moving forward. Every sentence you say is another image you're giving us. Your story is like an onion with many layers that you control in the peel-back reveal.

Here are the elements, wherever you choose to start, that you must remember and incorporate: C.R.O.W. This method was taught to me at my improv theater, Unexpected Productions, and is highly relevant in any storytelling arena. All of the brilliant teachers at this internationally recognized theater are trained to share this method for improv scenes, and it's absolutely applicable to live storytelling and any presentation.

C.R.O.W. STANDS FOR CHARACTERS, RELATIONSHIP,
OBJECTIVE, AND WHERE.

If you miss any one of the four core elements, you will have a wobbly three-legged table. Improvisers are magical because the actors are creating stories on the fly based on an audience suggestion, but there is a method to the magic. Follow C.R.O.W. As actors, we work diligently to make sure that *all* these elements are set up at the get-go to establish the story's track. The same goes for the presentation/storyteller who must paint a clear Business Mind Movie. So, here's where we follow the C.R.O.W. model. And there is no set order of how you work the C.R.O.W. into your story, that's the teller's choice, but here are some tips on how to infuse them into your story and keynotes.

KEEP THE TRAIN ON THE TRACKS AND AVOID THE WONDER / WANDER EFFECT

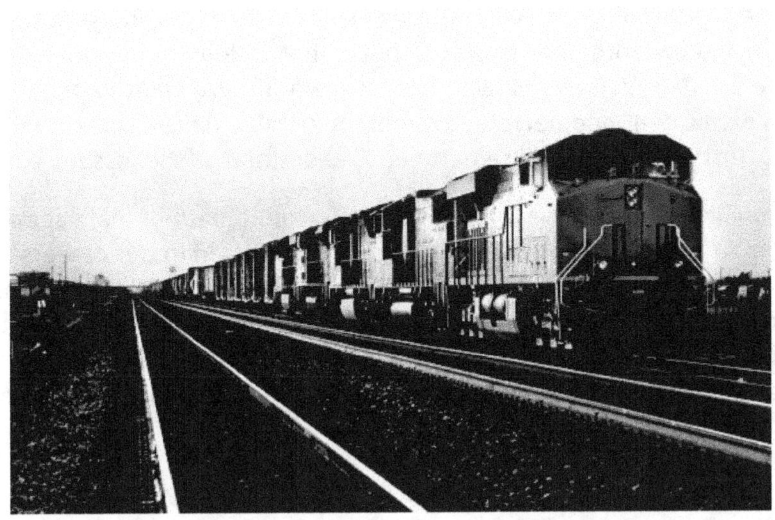

As the storyteller, if you are not clearly defining your C.R.O.W, your audience will start to get confused, and then they'll start to **wonder, then wander** off from listening to you. And with storytelling, if you wander off and try to jump back on the tracks, it's harder to catch up and follow the Mind Movie. When you say something that is vague, or use industry vernacular, you will instantly take listeners out of actively listening to you as they wander on the train tracks by themselves. That's why, as a storyteller, **you have an obligation to keep the communication train on the tracks,** moving forward at the right speed towards your "Aha!" and the reflection of the lesson learned. So how do you have C.R.O.W. keep the train on the tracks?

C.R.O.<u>W</u>.: START WITH THE WHERE—AND THERE'S A LOT TO THAT!

The WHERE is multi-faceted in your Mind Movie. Yes, it is the physical location, but it's also your age (or your character's age), which establishes your stage in life as well as their state of mind. Let's look at these more closely.

WHERE ARE YOU IN <u>AGE</u> AT THE TIME OF THE STORY?

This is important because the listener needs to imagine you or your key persona's stage in life. So, if you say, 'I was a kid when I first started my business.' *Okay...but were you six, twelve,*

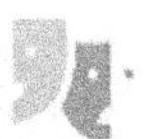

or seventeen? Big difference in how we'll see you. You can generalize if you're not sure but get us close. For example, you could say, *"I'm twenty-two years old, living in beautiful San Diego, and I'm broke. I've just graduated from college, moved out from Michigan to be with my boyfriend and palm trees, and I have no idea how to start my life as far as a career goes."*

Stating your age early in the story also allows the listeners to see you and understand you more vividly; they're climbing into your story. They can't help but imagine the storyteller at age twenty-two, and instantly that stage of life for most adults bubbles up. We were there. Most of us were still *Puppy Adults*, new to the "real world." We want to play, but sometimes, out of our own excitement and naivete, we metaphorically make a mess on the floor of life. And that's okay. Just clean it up and remember to keep calm as the lessons come.

Then again, many of us were headed down the linear lifepath of marriage and kids; some started earlier than that, and some of us felt lost and confused in our careers and compared ourselves to our supposedly "successful" friends who seemed to have the world by the tail already. We don't know that they *don't really have it yet*; they are also too young to know better; they are just better at playing the part. Those of us who have made it through our thirties understand this even better. Life comes in stages we measure as decades, and a lot of markers, or as "Life Chapters" (as explored earlier).

WHERE: DESCRIBE THE *PHYSICAL PLACE* AND GET INTO THE DETAILS.

Let's say your story starts outside. Was it a warm, sunny day at a beautiful park bustling with families all sitting together having picnics? The storyteller is completely in control of the set up scene's picture painting, and that train is sturdy on the tracks.

- It was a warm, sunny day
- at a beautiful park
- bustling with families all sitting together
- having picnics

Everyone knows the feeling of a warm, sunny day. Everyone has been to a beautiful park and seen families sitting together and have had or seen a picnic in action. The listener is on the ride with you. This scene literally feels pleasant, doesn't it?

Or

- I'm standing in an empty, creepy parking lot
- really wishing I had brought Chunk, my Pitbull, to protect me
- just in case...

Or

- I'm sitting in a stuffy, cramped office
- that smells like burnt coffee...

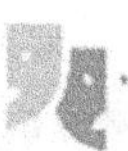

- When I see a cockroach scurry over my shoe
- Resisting the urge to gag…I know this job is not going to work for me.

Be aware that when you use general words, you're leaving a vague image in the listener's mind, making them work harder than they need to for your story. This goes back to the obligation you have as the Storyteller, to paint the images for them and entertain them as vividly as possible. If you don't provide the setup, they'll **Wonder/Wander** and that is not our desired outcome.

I often hear my new clients state one vague image after another, and it's there that I show them: "I see something, but not vividly….and it's not compelling enough for me to keep listening to you." Their faces usually get serious as the light bulb goes on.

WHERE ARE YOU *MENTALLY OR SPIRITUALLY*?

Your *state of mind* when you start your story is vitally important because we're moving towards a transformational "Aha!" so we must know your "before" from your "after." It doesn't have to be an extreme state of being because you don't operate on extreme emotion all the time. The story may start with a very normal, carefree moment before the inciting event occurs.

In Pradnya's story she was operating in a *business-as-usual* moment, helping her client just like she had done many times before. However, internally she was rooting for these two veterans to live out their dream, and she knew that the quote of $20K in attorney fees was going to be impossible for them to pay. So, when they rejected the plan and took a chance, "And my stomach **dropped** because *I knew you can't skip regulatory*," was the inciting event that would change all of their lives. As for Erin, she was in a *carefree, playful space* before receiving the news about her father-in-law being rushed to the hospital with a severe brain aneurysm.

C.R.O.W: CHARACTERS AND RELATIONSHIPS

Who was with you? All stories—including business stories— have characters and relationships. I see too many company case studies with no characters. The speaker will just vaguely say, "The Client" or "Corporation X" with no people to see and relate to. In life, *companies* are made of *buildings* that are filled with *people* who are *solving problems*—so get the *relevant people* players into your stories.

For example, starting a case story:

Cindy has been Senior Vice President of Sales for the past fifteen years. She's been at the company since the beginning, and today she's frustrated.

In just two sentences we now can imagine a person who has clout and credibility, and we know her state of mind in less than twenty-five words. Mind Movie started!

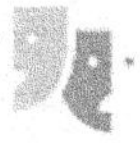

WHAT IS YOUR RELATIONSHIP TO EACH OTHER?

Have you known each other a long time? Maybe share a bit of history? Did you always like each other, or did you have a tumultuous past? Were you strangers? Did they seem warm and friendly and remind you fondly of someone you care about? Or were they terse and put you on edge? Think about how you felt and explore this as we inject it into your setup, describing the other person or people so we can *see* them. You also start drumming up a feeling of entertainment for the listener.

> *If the other person is an ally to your success, make us love them.*
> *If they play the nemesis, get us not to like them.*

Learn to catch yourself whenever you are saying things vaguely or colorlessly. For example, if you're telling a story about when you met your co-founder, avoid an opening like this: *We met at work. She was the manager, and I was the new potential hire. I liked her. She liked me too. She hired me.*

Do you tell stories like that or know someone who does? Me too. Right away, I'm asking myself *"Where were you working? How old were you? What did she look like? What impression did he have on you from the moment that you met him?"*

The bland description can take listeners out because they are, once again, going to **The Wonder/Wander Effect**. Your non-descriptive choices also make the listener work harder guessing the details. These are the details you want to find in your stories, especially the set up using C.R.O.W..

Here's an example of relationship set up that takes place early in my career. Watch how I'm setting the stage using C.R.O.W..

MY FIRST REAL JOB

I'm twenty-two years old. I'm a fresh adult. I'm so new in the world, there are eggshells behind my wet ears from my adult hatching. I need a job badly. Ready to fly the nest, but my wings are too wet to fly.

I walk into the San Diego warehouse office to interview for an advertising sales position. I have no idea what that position means, but she answered my pathetic resumé and still called me in. *Maybe I'm her playdough that she'll mold to a superstar?* I don't know, but I book the appointment.

The publisher is a petite woman in her fifties. Her name is Connie. I feel as though, in a prior career, she was probably the Assistant Principal that no one *ever* wanted to have to go

and see. She is rail thin, and when she sees me prance my twenty-two-year-old energy into her office, my long blonde hair flowing down my back and optimistic attitude that I am 'all that,' her eyebrow goes up. Her hazel eyes go dark, as she assesses my potential. *Should she just write me off?*

She stands up from her desk and offers a handshake. She squeezes my hand hard just so I know who the boss is. My attitude instantly changes, and I think, *Calm down. She means business.*

Do you like the boss at this stage? Maybe you do, maybe you don't know yet, but I'm planting seeds that our energy may not be aligned. Everyone has met that type of person so the story is already relatable to most people.

LIMIT YOUR CHARACTERS FOR YOUR LISTENER'S SAKE

As the storyteller, limit your characters to people that *only* add value to your story. If there was someone else there, but they were just standing in the room, you can feel free to edit them out of the story to keep it crisp. Remember, as the storyteller, you have power and obligation, so if you put a new person into your story, you must convince your listener that they need to be there, or your train will start to veer off the tracks. If you decide they need to be there, describe them in the same way you did with the main characters. If you mention them at the beginning but then never circle back to them, your listener is now **babysitting that character** in their minds; they'll want to know what happens to them. Why bother putting them in there if they add *nothing* to your story?

I've told a very poignant story about my grandmother's passing, and in reality, my father, my grandmother, and my sister were gathered around her deathbed. I chose not to include my sister in this particular story because she actually didn't say much at that sad moment. The *key moment* was between me and my dad and grandmother where I made a confession that I had borrowed money from my grandparents when I was dead broke in my early twenties. I was embarrassed and didn't want to disappoint my dad, and years later, at her deathbed, I confessed and apologized for not paying them back. Keeping my sister out of that moment allows for my listeners to handle the key three characters and not worry about the quiet one. So as the storyteller, while you remember your experiences, it's okay to edit down if it keeps your story clear and concise. As long as your story is true, you may craft it as you see fit to make for the best entertainment and your purpose of telling.

TREAT GROUPS OF PEOPLE LIKE A GREEK CHORUS

If you have a lot of people in a room during one of your stories, no need to name them all. That would overcrowd our minds. "The Team" or "The Group" can work just fine to keep

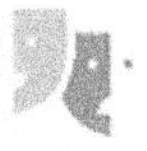

the train on the tracks. It's fun for the audience to also create their own band of background characters, so you don't have to take that all on as the storyteller. Let the audience create their own Mind Movies and fill in the blanks.

C.R.<u>O</u>.W.: OBJECTIVE STAKES

All stories must have stakes as mentioned earlier. Win or lose? Health or illness? Success or failure? If you don't have stakes, then you're really sharing an anecdote, which is fun and entertaining, but we want to share stories that tell the audience about the heart and soul of your business.

This next story example is a story in my library that I can share with young adults who are experiencing the Early Adult phase of life. It's a story of wisdom that uplifts and encourages the listener that "This too shall pass," so soak up the lessons while you can.

In the Connie story, the stakes are me getting the job and having an income so that I can pay my rent and put food on the table. Money will allow me to go out with friends and indulge in a movie, buy clothes, shed my baby chick feathers and grow real wings, and feel like a grown-up. Or, if I don't get the job, I'm back to the classifieds looking for another job, filling out more applications, getting more rejections, and feeling bad about myself.

I *need* this job!

MY FIRST REAL JOB, PART TWO

Connie politely asks me to sit down, and I pass her my resumé. It has very little to offer or impress with because it's really just a pad of my waitress and hostess jobs. At this point, I've just graduated from the University of Michigan with a bachelor's degree in General Studies. My boyfriend said, "I know what a BGS stands for: Big Grand Shit!" as he laughed. I replied "Or…Boyfriend Gone Soon."

He stopped laughing.

We need an Account Executive that will cold-call businesses in San Diego that want to support women-run businesses, and obviously get them to buy their products and services. You'll be paid commission *only*. I'm here to help you as you train. So, Melissa, why should I hire you?

This was my first interview question—and part of me wanted to say, *I have no freakin' idea. I've never done what you're asking.*

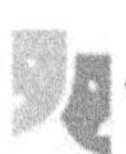

But Gut Instinct answers instead to help me out. As my lips utter words, I'm mesmerized by what is coming out of me All I can think is to just let it flow. Free fall with whatever Gut Instinct has to say as Melissa!

Connie: So, Melissa, why should I hire you for this ad sales job?

Gut Instinct: Well, in the restaurant world, I meet new people every fifteen minutes, so that in *a way* that moment is a cold call every time I walk up to the table. I don't know whether the patron will be in a good mood or bad, but I know they want something. So, I ask a few questions to find out what they are game for—make them feel that I'm friendly and knowledgeable about our food—and direct them onto the menu accordingly. I ask, listen, and then bring their food to them.

Connie looks at me and her dark hazel eyes start to lighten. She cocks her head, and I can see her visualizing me sitting at my own desk, on the phone, calling potential advertisers.

Gut Instinct: So, if I were to call on businesses, I suppose it's similar, but with more variety—like a buffet. I might be calling on a coffee shop who would love to have coffee business meetings from our readers—or a furniture store that would love to decorate the women's homes and offices. Essentially, I ask what they want, listen, and bring it to them in the form of an advertisement.

The lightbulb has gone off and my enthusiasm is back, along with joyous confidence. Connie sees it happening too. We are on the same page.

Gut Instinct: I'll be your Ad Waiter!

Connie: I'd like you to start on Monday. Please be here at 9:00 a.m.

The heaviness of worry immediately lifts and the excitement that I am now officially a working adult who will be able to make my parents proud has come to its fruition!

I learned that even though my past experiences don't completely match my current situation, I can find *something* using out-of-the-box thinking that meets the needs of whatever *the problem* is and seal the deal.

A story like this can be useful when you are hiring or recruiting or trying to get hired. Stories of work triumphs are imperative to add to your Story Library.

USING THESE TACTICS FOR A "PERSONAL" BUSINESS STORY

Tom Spann was one of my first clients for Story Fruition. He's a serial entrepreneur, having founded Accolade, a company that offers employers a solution for their employees who might be struggling with health insurance companies. It went IPO in 2020. Tom is now running Brightside—the same basic concept, but this is used when employees get buried under financial debt and burdens from a variety of life situations (divorce, health, ailing parent, etc.).

When it comes to numbers, data, and logical thinking, Tom thrives. The creative details, however, are what he finds more challenging, so he hired me. He is an evolved man and can take an honest look at himself and say, "I don't think, when it comes to public speaking, that I'm that dynamic. I rely on charts and graphs that interest me, but that doesn't work for the whole room. Please help me improve."

We worked together for six months as I story-mined his own Story Fruition because, as CEO, Tom needs to show investors and clients that he not only understands the science of the business he is building, but also be likeable and relatable. He must communicate *why* Brightside deserves funding in order to help his target audience. His ability to captivate his audience comes through his storytelling as he weaves these elements into his presentations. Here is a sample of Tom's own story that can introduce a lot about his character on a variety of levels. Watch for C.R.O.W.

"YOU FIGURE IT OUT"
TOM'S FINANCIAL STORY FRUITION

I am seventeen years old and sitting at the dining-room table with my father, finishing up our scrambled egg breakfast. He unexpectedly pulls out a folder and pushes a few pieces of paper across the table towards me and says, "These are my financials. You figure out how you can go to college and how I can pay for it."

My dad is a proud military man who held decent jobs in sales and marketing roles in the industrial oil business sector. My mother, his wife of twenty years, is an elementary school teacher whose wages all went to pay for the school supplies for their four kids: me and my three younger sisters. And, like a lot of people, my parents fell prey to the 'Keeping up with the Jones' Syndrome.'

We lived in a nice house next to a golf course, ate at nice restaurants, and drove decent cars. Everything looked great on the surface, but now I could see that my dad was actually buried in debt. Drowning in it. And adding college tuition to this pit didn't appear to be in the cards. I had never imagined not going to college, so this was a shock. But somehow in that moment, I felt empathy for my dad and just said, "I'll take a look at this and get back to you."

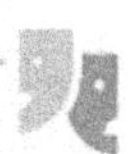

Yes, I was equally surprised at how adult I sounded. The truth was I didn't know how the hell I'd make this work.

So, I did research. I learned about colleges "in-state" to keep tuition down. Once I had my plan, I cut a deal with my dad. "If I get the tuition covered, could you please cover my food costs?" He smiled and exhaled and said 'yes.'

I was off and rolling, but still not sure how to make it all work. I applied for financial aid. I got two jobs while I went to school. One was a work-study program in finance, the other was managing the Faculty Club Banquets, which is where I learned how to manage people and lots of moving parts. As a perk, I also got free dinners, so that saved my struggling parents more on food money.

This worked well until my senior year when my dad had to have an emergency root canal, and my little sister wrecked the car. She was fine, but these two bills were devastating to us. I feared that I couldn't finish my senior year, but I decided to take a risk. I wrote a letter to the university and shared what was happening and that I needed a $1500 loan to finish my senior year, or I'd have to leave. They looked at my grades and record and had seen me bussing tables at their banquets. They wrote back and said, "Here, we'll just give you the $1500." It blew me away. To get help without any expectation of repayment. I have since repaid them with interest and proud to have done so.

I graduated with about $45,000 in debt; today that's about $100K, but I figured it out in life and paid it off. And even better, so did my dad, with his own debt. I suppose we ended up growing up together.

Give your reflection at the end. Tell us the lesson.

This is why I understand the people we help at Brightside. Sometimes life just tosses things at us. And we need help because we don't know how to navigate through it by ourselves. That's the secret...you don't have to manage it alone. I'm grateful my dad was honest and brave enough to share the real situation with me. I know he was embarrassed and ashamed. But it became a part of our journey in life and that's what makes us who we are as people. Our trials and tribulations. It's the humility and gratitude of receiving, and the joy of giving, that makes it all worth it.

—Tom Spann, CEO/Founder, Brightside

Tom's Story Fruition shows vulnerability and humanity, and that draws the audience in because of his willingness to expose the challenges that he's had to overcome. And that those very experiences were the pathways to his current career success. He proceeded to work with Story Fruition to help him with his big Andreessen Horowitz investor presentation, wove

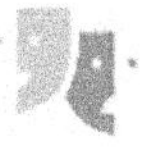

in several well-crafted and emotional case stories, and landed $35M in Series A funding. It was an honor to be a part of his journey to this success.

As an entrepreneur, a business leader or visionary, tell your own story. Dive back into your life and look for childhood moments that had an influence on your character today. *What values did your family teach you that you now use in your own life?*

CHAPTER EIGHT

MAKE US SEE IT, HEAR IT, SMELL IT, TASTE IT AND FEEL IT!

Professional storytellers know that tapping into the senses is the *key* to great storytelling for any Mind Movie, and it's the most fun. This is where the details will paint the images in your listeners' minds. What is magical about storytelling is that you have the power to alter these images by simple word choices, changing and controlling their emotional connection to your story. You become the puppet master.

All five senses are available to you to tap into when telling your stories, and the more you bring them in, the more captivating your storytelling skills become. People cannot help but lean into your words, your energy, your tonalities, and your pace and pausing. Let's look at the power of each one of the senses and share some examples of how to use them for maximum impact.

Engage the Senses

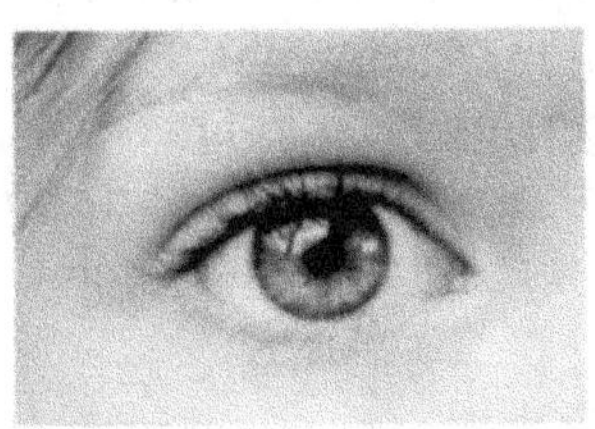

SIGHT

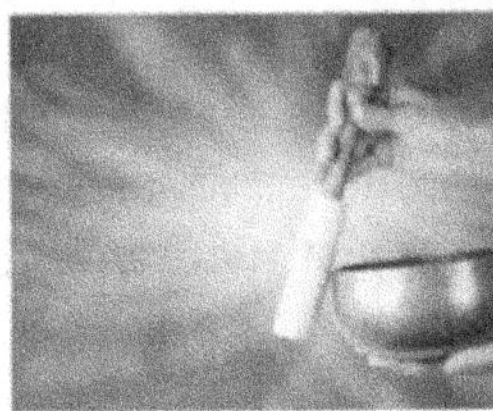

SOUND

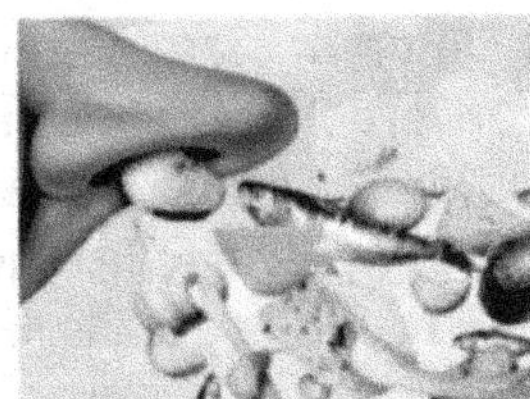

SMELL

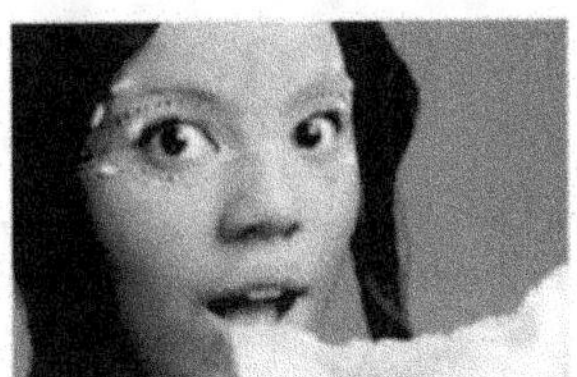

TASTE

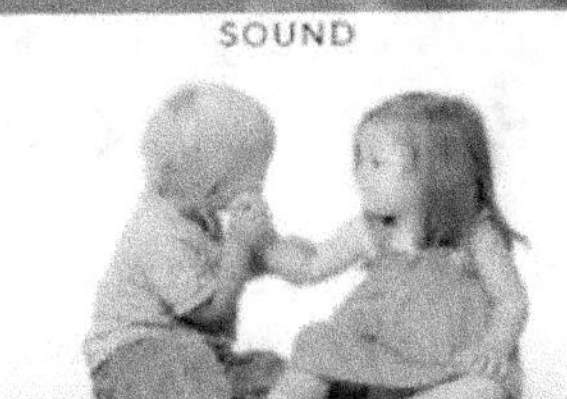

FEEL (TOUCH & EMOTIONS)

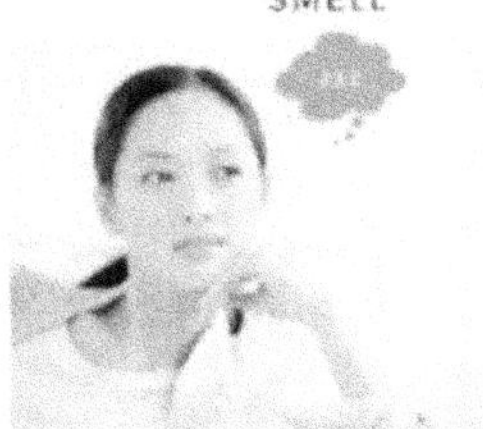

THOUGHTS

SIGHT

Show us the scene, don't just tell us.

"I'm driving down the road with my dad."

That's telling us. I can see it, but it's vague and not exciting. Try this:

"It's a sunny Sunday morning and I'm with my dear dad. We're flying down a country backroad in his red convertible."

That's showing us. That moves from rhetoric to Mind Movie Making. Where did the details that paint the image go?

1. **Sunny, Sunday Morning:** We can see and feel the weather and some may even feel the warmth of the sun. Putting in the detail of Sunday can create a mood for the listeners. It's a weekend day and most people are trying not to work. We are in a more suspended mental space to relax and do what we want on a Sunday. And sometimes that is just doing nothing at all, but to go on a nice drive.
2. **A country backroad:** Instantly we are off the main freeway (if that's where the listener unconsciously placed you) and that creates images of things like open fields, farms, or maybe mountains and lakes. That's up to the listeners, but the country road is much different than a city highway. The road itself may instantly change to a dirt road and that changes their Mind Movie.
3. **Red convertible** says a lot. First it pops color into our heads, and a convertible offers a different state of mind than an SUV or a station wagon. Also, what does this red convertible say about Dad? Is he fun and playful? Is he driving his mid-life crisis car, or his dream-come-true mobile? We don't know yet, but those questions and thoughts are popping into listener's minds. In just *two sentences*, that much is happening when you fill in the details like this!

WATCH HOW ONE CHANGE CAN CHANGE EVERYTHING

What if I said, "In Dad's dinged-up, filthy convertible that he just can't seem to let go of." How does that change your feelings or impression about Dad and my attitude and relationship to him?

EASILY SHOW THE RELATIONSHIP USING YOUR VOICE AND TONE

What are our states of mind?? Playful? Serious? This will become clear in my oratory delivery. If I have an upbeat tone in my voice, then yes, playful. But if I say it slowly and imply that Dad's out of control...that changes the entire Mind Movie as well as the listeners' opening emotional experience.

> *Your voice, your pace, your words all enhance the Mind Movie when it comes to oratory storytelling.*

SMELLS

Engaging the olfactory sparks listener connection. Adding familiar smells sends us into our own memories, and when your listener says, "I remember when...." that is a huge compliment for you as a storyteller because they are engaging with you. In the earlier story about Dr. Data and Sarah, the cancer patient, there's a key moment that is soft but packs emotional punch:

Sarah looks over at the Christmas tree. She sees some pine needles on the beige carpet. Normally that would irritate her, and she'd go vacuum...but right now...she just wants to smell that pine.

Hard not to smell the pine—even if you do not celebrate this holiday, most of us have seen a Christmas tree and smelled pine. The listener won't know what you're doing, but you are seducing their imagination because you are the storyteller, and you have the power.

You can also use smells that aren't fun. In one of my stories that played on NPR, "WAKING UP," I am describing a moment in life when at twenty-three years old, I found myself in the middle of a San Diego Psychic Ring. It's a funny story of bravery after acute gullibility. In this story, I play with smells literally and figuratively:

I'm twenty-three years old and standing outside my new apartment in San Diego. My boyfriend, Bill, had broken up with me. He literally just disappeared overnight, and I am confused, angry, upset, and heartbroken. So, I do what any normal, level-headed person does: I seek to find a psychic to get Bill back. I find an ad in the newspaper that says: *"Find Love & Money In Your Life. Call Sonia, The Psychic."*

So, I call her and book an appointment for the next day. When I walk into her dimly lit parlor, it smells of burnt incense and fresh desperation.

One of my favorite storytellers is my friend, Kory May, from Iowa City, Iowa. (Go, Hawks!) He always does a brilliant job of weaving smells into his stories. When he describes a family picnic memory, your mouth waters for BBQ ribs and burgers off the grill. You can taste the lemon pies that his mother baked. As I listen, I can see it, taste it, smell it. He's a marvelous storyteller. Or in another more serious story, Kory is standing in line at a Christmas Eve Food Bank.

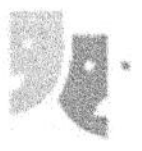

> As I gaze at the people in line for their free, warm meal, I smell the savory green bean casserole and roasted chicken, and then the smell of a pungent wet diaper from the baby being held in her disheveled mother's arms. The irony that one place can smell like comfort and misfortune all at once.

Play with the smells in your story—they are unexpected and often delight your listener as you add one more layer to your story experience.

TASTE

When you engage the nose, you will often engage the tastebuds, so play with it. This can make your story sweet, sour, or savory simply by the words you choose. Once again, this element is both literally and figuratively powerful.

I have another Story Fruition client who is an amazing entrepreneur dedicated to allergy-sensitive customers as well as sustainable and ethical ingredient sourcing. Phebe Rossi started NuFlours Bakery in Seattle, and her products are now distributed throughout the Pacific Northwest, and soon nationally. She's an entrepreneur changing the baking world. As we developed her own Story Fruition, she shared that due to her own allergies as a child growing up on a farm in eastern Washington State, she was often stuck inside to avoid the wheat and dust because they'd cause breathing difficulties and uncomfortable rashes. This is before science had caught up, and we had started to understand the power of food over certain people's nervous systems, as well as the power of food as medicine.

Phebe had *no choice* but to learn how to cope on her own. One way she did this was by baking chocolate chip cookies for her and her sisters' lunches. And this is where she started to experiment with baking and the science of it.

COOKIES

My sisters are outside baling hay. I'm eight years old and stuck inside again. I hate working outside because my skin breaks out into one big burning rash. So, baking is my favorite "chore." Baking is the friend that I turn to for comfort and a creative outlet.

Creaming the butter carefully with the brown and white sugars until it's both smooth and gritty. The farm fresh eggs and vanilla go next. Each one is changing the aroma inside the stainless-steel bowl as I'm stirring. Next, I add the sifted flour, baking soda, and salt, and gradually the sandy butter starts to smooth. Then the best part: pouring in the semi-sweet chocolate chips—the smell of the cookie dough instantly changes again. It's irresistible. I scoop up some raw dough and savor every morsel.

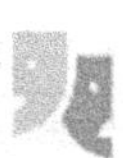

Twelve minutes later, I pull the hot chocolate-chip cookies out of the oven. I watch them deflate as the cool air does its magic. In a few minutes, the outsides will stay crunchy, and the middle soft and chewy. As I bite into one, I feel the melted chocolate rest on my tongue. This is pure happiness. I learned early that baking was my passion. And I want everyone to be able to enjoy delicious baked good as much as possible, despite allergies.

—Phebe Rossi, Founder/CEO, NuFlours Bakery

Okay…Okay…That was delicious! We'll wait for you to whip up your own batch of cookies and return to this book while they're baking.

SOUNDS

Now that we have our eyes, nose and tastebuds ignited, let's tickle the ears. We can use sounds to animate many things in storytelling. When I'm telling the Dr. Data story live, I always make a "PING!" sound when he darts away from me. The audience giggles because it's an unexpected, but well-placed sound due to its slight cartoon effect. Play with juxtaposed words to delight your listeners.

I walk into the employee lunchroom, a place where employees typically relax and enjoy **friendly banter** on their lunch breaks. But this lunchroom had nothing like that happening. The tables were empty except for lunch boxes placed to mark "territory" for when their owners would return for lunch. **The quiet screamed out at me**: This place is not a healthy work environment.

Or, back to Sarah and Dr. Data:

Sarah looks over at the Christmas tree. She sees some pine needles on the beige carpet. Normally that would irritate her, and she'd go vacuum…but right now…she just wants to smell that pine.

Did you hear the vacuum?

As you use the senses to infuse layers into your Mind Movie, you're stimulating all those delicious story-listening receptors in your brain to produce oxytocin, endorphins, and dopamine (plus others), creating a soup of emotions that transport you and your listeners to new places.

THE POWER OF DIALOGUE TO BOLSTER MORE SOUND INTO YOUR STORYTELLING

In my opinion, the best place to have sound is in *dialogue*. I would say that dialogue opportunities are the most missed opportunities by many storytellers, especially when they are new

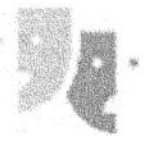

at it. That's because it's vulnerable for the storyteller to actually step away from themselves and *into* the scene. Dialogue between characters *shows* the audience so much more than just telling them the dialogue.

> *It's entertaining when the Storyteller shifts in and out of being the narrator to one of the characters in the scene, using the potent power of dialogue.*

Read that sentence again, please. That's the trick to your Mind Movie. Two characters are established and then they talk. They come alive and enrich the Mind Movie instantly. Here's the novice way of doing it:

I meet the manager and he tells me that he has concerns about work safety on the factory floor.

OR...use dialogue to bring the character alive in your story:

I meet Bruce, the factory floor manager. He's been with the company for only five years, but this gentleman is aware of the lack of safety protocols in place, and he constantly worries about his team. He chokes up and says, "We are expected to just keep pushing these people, and they are not equipped with safety or appreciation. I don't have the resources to support my team like they desperately need. No one is recognized, only told to work harder, faster..."

As I listen to him, I now see why I didn't hear friendly sounds in the lunchroom.

How different does this story become simply by adding more details using the dialogue? As a professional storyteller, I step fully into the scene and the characters, adjusting my voice, tone, and pacing to make the scenes come alive. I'm not worried that people might think I'm weird for being animated. And if they do, well, I'm okay with it. Storytelling can also break down barriers that you may have built. Push yourself to new heights and you'll find that your listeners enjoy what you have to say more, and as the Storyteller, you'll have a lot more fun with it too!

I love to use full dialogue whenever possible because it adds textures and dimensions to my stories. If you go onto my site, StoryFruition.com, under **Melissa's Storytelling**, I host my work. Take a listen to *"Life is Like a Waiter"* where I clearly play the voices of my parents to differentiate between them and add layers to my Mind Movie. Now this story is a personal story—not likely used in business – but you never know. It may be helpful if I were doing a talk about grief recovery for the National Alliance of Mental Illness, so this is why I'm bringing it forward. If you watch it, study the use of dialogue and characters that are woven throughout the piece.

WHAT ABOUT ACCENTS?

Most of us in Storytelling Land say to avoid accents, *especially* if you have no connection at all to that culture. You'll just look like you're making fun of them or even appear racist. In most cases it is inappropriate, and your Human Resources director will fall out of their chair if that gets back to them. And, sorry to say it, but most people do a shoddy job at accents, so you'll only just add to your troubles and take your listeners out of active listening. Not everyone has the talent of Robin Williams, who is famous for his hilarious story about the Scottish and their invention of the game of golf. He was an *exception* to the rule.

I was in a storytelling grand slam and a very white man started to imitate an Indian woman in his story by doing a mockery dance of her culture and using her accent (poorly). My fellow storytellers and I were all on Instant Messenger and the boards lit up. "What is he doing?!" One of our tellers is Indian, and she said, "Not okay." It was so uncomfortable, and horrifying, that multiple complaints hit the advisory board. The next day an email went out to say that, "Unless it is your own family's accent, we ask that you not include it in your story."

I am comfortable doing my parents' and grandparents' Oklahoma accents because I am aware that these main characters have been fully developed over decades. I use the accents to simply bring my characters to life for my listeners. But if someone else did my mother's accent in one of my stories, well, unless you're my sister, knock it off!

TOUCH/FEEL

Here's where more dimensions can occur in great storytelling: touch and feel, physically, emotionally, and/or spiritually. Play with this sense as much as you can.

TACTILE

- He shook my hand. It felt like sandpaper. This man has carried many hammers in his life.
- Her hand felt soft like silk as I admired her delicate pink fingernail polish.
- My confidence felt like a calm lake, no rippled nerves to distract me.
- When my boss hugged the new employee, she stiffened like an emery board. I felt awkward watching it.

TOUCH EMOTIONALLY:

- My heart smiled broadly when he said, "You've won the deal!"

TOUCH SPIRITUALLY:

After my divorce, I went through a period of natural depression and just sat on the couch licking my wounds like an injured cat. I started to write and images of cicadas popped in (probably Gut Instinct taking over my pen) and I wrote:

I feel like a cicada shedding off its seventeen-year-old protective armor. It is preventing me from living my dreams. I am now ready to hatch out and throw that old armor to the ground. I don't need it anymore. And now, with my new, pure *soul body*, and my clear, *conscious* eyes…I see the world for what I want it to be. And my wings? These wings are so much stronger at fifty-five than they could ever have been at twenty-five. I'm embracing my metamorphosis, and fly as high as possible to happiness.

THOUGHTS

In acting, there is something called "the fourth wall," and it's an imaginary wall between the actors and the audience. It's as if the audience is behind "something" and looking into the life of the characters on stage. Shakespeare broke "the fourth wall" and created characters that let you know how they *really* felt about a situation by talking directly to the audience. Allowing the listeners to get inside your head and hear your own inner monologue is a crowd pleaser. You are really getting intimate with them if you play this wonderful element into your stories. However, you must be very clear when you are doing it because you can confuse the listener if it's not done properly—then off the tracks the train doth roll.

As mentioned earlier, I tell a comedic personal story, "The Santa Game," where my children serve my derriere on a silver platter. The scene is rich in dialogue, character, and inner monologue. When you see anything *italicized* that is the inner monologue. Here's an excerpt from the story:

> My mother was the best at the holidays. Every single one was a full event from home décor to the big meal. However, she had one serious rule: "I don't lie to my kids! Santa Claus is a big lie and I won't do it. That present you're holding— that's from me and your Daddy."
>
> Her honesty rule worked too. I knew that she was playing games with me as the Easter Bunny, the Tooth Fairy, and of course, Santa. I felt bad for my second-grade friends who were fully buying into the illusion. *Didn't they question the facts? How can a guy in a hot-red suit fly in the air— in a sleigh— led by flying reindeers—in one night— and jump down the chimney—for every kid—in the world? Where was the soot?*

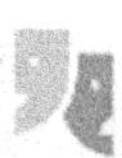

They believed it because they believed their parents. Their parents wouldn't lie to them. No way.

Yes way.

So, I made the same decision as my wise mother and followed suit; I would not lie to my kids about these fables.

Almost three decades pass and I'm thirty-six years old and I'm now a hip and cool Gen X new mother living in the Pacific Northwest. My first "spawn," Quincy, is three years old and sitting in their messy bedroom. Stuffed animals and puzzles are all over the floor when Quincy asks out of nowhere:

"Mommy, if I'm a good kid, will I be on Santa's nice list?"

Here it is...here is my time to set the record straight!

"Honey....Santa is just a...."

Quincy stops me by holding up their chubby little hand and says slowly, "Mommy...if I am a good kid, will I be on Santa's Nice List?"

What's happening? Are they giving me orders? Q's an old soul, I know this.... but I don't know how to play the Santa Game! OOOOOH....wait a second.... all the cul-de-sac moms have told me you can get stuff done with the Santa Lure. I could get the house cleaned; the dog walked...

Then I hear my mother's voice say, "Missy, don't do it! Don't lie to your kid!"

Oh, I'm going to do it, Mother...I'm lying...I mean playing!

I turn to my beautiful child and look deep into Quincy's innocent blue eyes and say, "Yes. Yes, honey. If you are a good kid, you'll be on Santa's Nice List."

"Okay!" says Quincy with delight.

Really? My kid is believing me?

"So, let's start with your toys right now. Please pick them up and tidy your room."

"Okay!"

Oh....this is good. This is GOOD! I'm going to get stuff done!

I then used the Santa Lure all year round. "You better walk the dog, if you wanna be on Santa's Nice List!"

"Okay!" as Quincy takes Tulip, our black Labrador, out to the backyard.

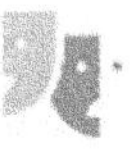

"You better brush your teeth two times a day, 'cuz (whispered) Santa and the Tooth Fairy are best friends, and you don't want to give the Tooth Fairy a gross rotten tooth to pick up. That's icky."

"Okay!" and Quincy spits Crest into the sink.

The dog is walked, the house is clean. I am getting stuff done via my kid. Things are working beautifully.

Then, one night, we are sitting at the kitchen table enjoying our Kraft macaroni and cheese when Quincy says, "Mommy....you're Santa."

WHAT?! WHERE DID THIS COME FROM?

"What? No, no I'm not!"

"Yes, you are. You're Santa....the Easter Bunny....and I think the Tooth Fairy too."

My heart splits. I am mortified that I have been busted *and yet, very impressed that Quincy has figured this out on their own by five years old. Way above the curve. Old Soul stuff.* And, I learned that my mother was right. Lying wasn't what I wanted to do as a parent. So, our Santa Game ended.

THE SANTA GAME AS A BUSINESS STORY?

Maybe. I could use this personal and relatable parenting tale in a keynote to show the flurry of cause and effect. Perhaps a hot-shot salesperson who shoots first and apologizes later could be juxtaposed with this Santa Game parenting choice. I'm clearly going selfishly along to get what I want: the house cleaned, and the dog walked. Sometimes in start-ups, an eager salesperson might overstate the technology's capability, but eventually the client figures out the sales game.

> *"A fool thinks himself to be wise, but a wise man knows himself to be a fool."*
> —William Shakespeare

I hope that this chapter resonates with you because it will transform your storytelling skills. When we get them to see it, taste it, smell it, hear it, and feel it, your brain's parietal lobe (located in the cerebral cortex) gets involved in two ways as a listener. It feels sensation and perception and the integration and interpretation of sensory information. So, as the Mind Movie Maker weaving in the senses, you have your audience in the palm of your hands. They are leaning into you, Storyteller!

CHAPTER NINE

ADVANCE AND EXPAND

I hear this almost every day in my work with clients: "My stories are not interesting, and I take forever to get to the point" or "I tell the story so quickly that I see my listener gets bored or confused." Those statements come right back to simply learning how to use a clean Story Arc towards your "Aha!" with a balance of advancing and expanding.

HOOK US FROM THE BEGINNING

As stated earlier, the Storyteller is the conductor keeping the train on the communication tracks. Your plot points advance the story. But along the way, you may want to stop in a specific scene and expand on the details to entertain and inform the listeners.

All stories need **expansion,** meaning that as the Teller, you're stopping to establish key characters and give details that solidify the Mind Movie. Most people derail here. They advance too much and deny the story the ability to vividly unfold, creating vague images and little emotional investment. Or, sometimes, they expand way too much, and the listener gets antsy about "Get to the point!" Have you ever met someone who drones on and on and on... and when they're done, you just want to ask for that five minutes of your life back? Like a bag of fire-hot cheese puffs, their story was just empty calories.

Balance. It's all about balance.

So, let's return to the Story Arc to further illustrate this point and to plot out Tom's story and look at advance and expand moments.

Your Story of Transformation

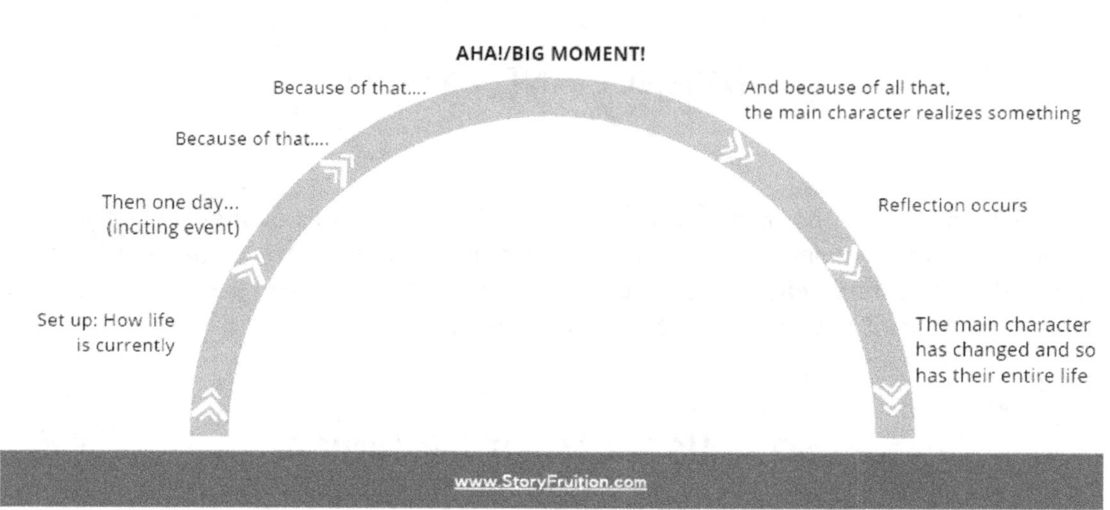

BREAKFAST OF UN-CHAMPIONS

I am seventeen years old and sitting at the dining room table with my father, finishing up our scrambled egg breakfast.

EXPANSION: INTRODUCE YOUR CHARACTERS AND LIFE IS CURRENTLY

My dad is a proud military man who held decent jobs in sales and marketing roles in the industrial oil business sector. My mother, his wife of twenty years, is an elementary school teacher whose wages all went to pay for the school supplies for their four kids: me and my three younger sisters. And, like a lot of people, my parents fell prey to the 'Keeping up with the Jones' Syndrome.' We live in a nice house next to a golf course, eat at nice restaurants, and drive decent cars.

ADVANCE: INCITING EVENT

As I'm eating my eggs and reading the newspaper, Dad unexpectedly pulls out a folder and pushes a few pieces of paper across the table towards me and says, "These are my financials. You figure out how you can go to college and how I could pay for it."

EXPANSION: SHOW THE RELATIONSHIP AND REACTION TO THE INCITING EVENT

As I look at his bills, I see we are drowning in debt. And adding college tuition to this didn't appear to be on the cards. I had never imagined not going to college, so this was a shock. But somehow in that moment, I felt empathy for my dad and just said, "I'll take a look at this and get back to you."

Yes, I was equally surprised at how adult I sounded. The truth was, I didn't know how the hell I'd make this work.

ADVANCE: BECAUSE OF THAT...

So, I researched. I learned about colleges in state to keep tuition down. Once I had my plan, I cut a deal with my dad. "If I get the tuition covered, could you please cover my food costs?" He smiled and exhaled and said 'yes.'

ADVANCE: BECAUSE OF THAT...

I was off and rolling, but still not sure how to make it all work. I applied for financial aid. I got two jobs while I went to school.

EXPANSION:

One was a work-study program in finance; the other was managing the Faculty Club Banquets, which is where I learned how to manage people and lots of moving parts. As a perk, I also got free dinners, so that saved my struggling parents more on food money.

ADVANCE: ANOTHER INCITING EVENT

This worked well until my senior year when my dad had to have an emergency root canal, and my little sister wrecked the car. She was fine, but these two bills were devastating to us.

EXPANSION:

I feared that I wouldn't be able to finish my senior year, but I decided to take a risk. I wrote the university a letter and shared what was happening and that I needed a $1500 loan to finish my senior year, or I'd have to leave. They looked at my grades and record and had seen me bussing tables at their banquets. They wrote back and said "Here, we'll just give you the $1500."

AHA! MOMENT

It blew me away. To get help without any expectation of repayment. I have repaid them as an alumni with interest and proud to have been able to do so.

ADVANCE: BECAUSE OF THAT CHANGE IN ME...

I graduated with about $45,000 in debt; today that's about $100K, but I figured it out in life and paid it off. And even better, so did my dad with his own debt. I suppose we both grew up together.

REFLECTION: POINT OF THE STORY WHERE WISDOM IS SHARED AS THE "NEW YOU"

This is why I understand the people we help at Brightside. Sometimes life just tosses things at us. And we need help but don't know how to navigate through it by ourselves. That's the secret...you don't have to do it alone.

I'm grateful that my dad was honest and brave enough to share the real situation with me. I know he was embarrassed and ashamed, but it became part of our journey in life and that's what makes us who we are as people. Our trials and tribulations. It's the humility and gratitude of receiving, and the joy of giving, that makes it all worth it.

—Tom Spann, Founder/CEO, Brightside

That's PODCAST GOLD! This story could be used in a variety of business situations. When Tom gets asked any common questions such as the following, for example, he can pull this story out of his own Story Library to shine. When asked any of these questions in an interview, Tom could tell this story.

- **Why do you do this work?**

- How did you get into the world of finance?
- What moments in your life jump out at you as moments that revealed your creativity/resilience/cooperation/fear of the unknown/understanding the client's plight?

This story works because it shows a personal and vulnerable time in Tom's life that changed him. It put him on his trajectory towards finance and entrepreneurship. He has clearly defined characters, and only a few (Dad, Little Sister, Mom, and the Dean) who show up momentarily to move the story along. Tom goes on the journey with him as we get to know **his true character**. After hearing this story, what opinions do you formulate about him as a leader?

A) Do you like him?
B) Can you see he gets things done without compromising on either empathy or logic?
C) Would you trust him?
D) And will you remember his story?
E) All of the above?

The last question is vital because as the Storyteller, if he delivers the story with authenticity while he paints the images in your head, he has done what all stories hope to do:

The ultimate goal is to be remembered and appreciated for what your story teaches.

CHAPTER TEN

TIME TRAVEL

Let's talk more about the art of time travel in storytelling. To do it properly without confusing your listeners where you are in time, you must be deliberate and clear, making sure the train is on the communication tracks and not derailed. Have you listened to someone who's jumping all over the place in their life and you can't keep up? Just as you *think* you understand, they jump to another era of their life and your confusion returns? Time leaps into the future, back to the past, then back to the now takes crafting and concentration.

In many stories, you may leap forward or backwards in time, and this is where you need to be clear. You may be an adult in the beginning of the story, but then something happens and you "suddenly flash back" to when you were six years old. We must know where you are in time – at all times! So here are some tips on how to achieve this advanced level of storytelling, which will differentiate you from mediocre storytellers.

BE DELIBERATE WITH YOUR AGE AND AVOID MAKING YOUR LISTENER DO THE MATH.

My storytelling style, when it comes to time leaps, is to be direct with your age out of the gate in a story. The listener needs to place you immediately in life, so state something like:

"It's 1981, I'm sixteen years old and worried about college applications...."

Great! Your story is starting off nicely. Right away, we know who you are and your state of mind. But then you fast forward in time, and you have a couple of choices when it comes to indicating that leap.

By twenty-four years old, I've lived more life than I had expected to. (Good.)
vs
Eight years later, I've lived more life than I had expected to. (Meh.)

The second choice involves math. So, you were sixteen + eight years= twenty-four years old. It's your choice whether you want to use this style of storytelling, but you will momentarily lose some people as you make them calculate your age. I advise that you just make it *easy* and tell the listener how old you are, and the listener can just say in their heads, "Some time has passed."

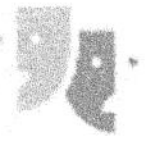

Here's an example of a Story Fruition by Dr. Noor Ali, CEO of DrNoorHealth.com. As you read or listen to her story, watch how we state her age and time travel in her life as she twists and turns to go from being a highly successful surgeon in Bangladesh, to a health insurance sales CEO. There are stakes, time travel, rich, recurring characters, and it all happens in less than five minutes of her outstanding storytelling that she shares in many podcast interviews.

THE PATH LESS TRAVELLED

I'm five years old and I'm sitting on my grandfather's lap. I lovingly call him Dada. We're reading our favorite book together. It's *Gray's Anatomy*, the number one medical textbook for medical students worldwide. I've got hearts in my eyes as I look up at my "Dada" and he looks sweetly down to me and says, "You're going to be a doctor just like me one day, aren't you?" And I say, "Yes, Dada, I am!"

The wheels are in motion. My educational trajectory is fast tracked and propelled into a track towards medicine. In middle school, I'm taking high school courses; in high school, I'm done taking advanced college courses. I'm eighteen years old, about to start my college career in medicine, living in the Big Apple, when I get a phone call...

"Hello?"

"Dada...died."

"What?!"

My father looks at all of us and says, "We all have to move back to Bangladesh *now*!"

Before I know it, I'm standing in the 118-degree sweltering heat in the middle of my all-women's medical college in Bangladesh clutching my own copy of *Gray's Anatomy* and I'm tripping over chicken and goats. In New York City, I'd be eating that chicken from a halal chicken and rice cart!

"Dada, where are you?!"

My world is upside down. I'm too skinny because I can't eat the food. I can't communicate with my peers due to the language barrier. I'm struggling just to survive. The only thing that brings me comfort is my education. So, I dive in deep.

One of my professors notices my talent and says, "Wow! You just timed a C-section at 16:30 seconds. No one has ever done that before!"

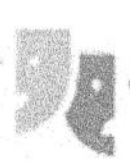

I was on a roll. In my "free" time, I founded an internationally award-winning community project that served free prenatal care to slum-dwelling women all over Bangladesh. My work was recognized on the stage of the United Nations in 2014.

I'm twenty-three years old, in my final year of medical school, and LOVE was the LAST thing on my mind. A man that I had met six years earlier in New York City finds me halfway across the globe. He asks my father if we can go on a date?

My father says, "Sure, if you'll marry her."

"Okay...can I have time to think about it?"

"Sure, I'll give you fifteen minutes."

That was on a Wednesday, by Friday evening, we were married. That road showed up pretty quickly, but I took it, and I never looked back.

The beginning of the road is rocky, filled with uneven potholes, long-distance relationship strain, but I'm thriving in my surgical career.

Two years go by, and it's time to return to NYC to be with my husband.

The road gets rockier. I was a superstar surgeon in Bangladesh, but in order to practice surgery in the United States, I HAVE to pass the United States Medical Licensing Exam. On paper, I'm just a high school graduate.

I'm mopping floors at my first job in the US at a Subway sandwich shop and all I can think about is this exam. To me, this exam is like an enormous fire-breathing dragon. I'm terrified. And the heat of the pressure to pass this test is melting my armor.

I finally get my results back, and it's not what I expected. I missed it. By one question. Now what am I going to do? My path just changed again.

PAUSE.

Hello, Sunny Florida!

I'm twenty-six years old and living with my new in-laws. I'm trying out different careers, but nothing makes me feel worthy until this opportunity for health insurance presents itself. *Hmmm...health insurance, they never taught this in medical school, let me take a look*. I grab it and dive in deeper. In my second week of training, I'm handed this medical underwriting guide.

Amy, next to me, is googling and stumbling over terminologies like Cole-cys-tec-tomy?

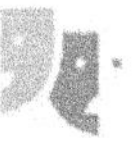

I respond easily, "It's cholecystectomy- resection of the gallbladder. Indicated in cholelithiasis and some cases of chronic cholecystitis."

It's like I'm reading *Gray's Anatomy* again and I'm FLUENT in this language!

And that's when I knew that my road had just merged into my path. My medical career, my understanding of global health care systems, and now my experience in health insurance were now coming together to create the new Dr. Noor Healthcare Advisor, my very own personal brand!

Since then, I have recreated the customer experience journey for purchasing health insurance. Using my insider's lens, I work with trailblazing entrepreneurs to access quality and customizable health care plans. The value I bring to the table is my clinical know-how so I can instantly assess what coverage you need, and sometimes even more importantly, what you don't need.

I've travelled on many roads less traveled, but I have always trusted in myself that I will figure things out—and that's the richness of life!

—Dr. Noor Ali, CEO, DrNoorHealth.com

Since we crafted her own Story Fruition together, Noor uses it in her podcast interviews and her social marketing, breaking it into three "acts" that leave cliff-hangers for the interviewer to discuss and deepen her message. **Play with the time era.**

I love to use time travel in most of my stories, and I've learned ways to do it so it's clear and concise. When you time travel, you will want to pick up elements of that era to make that time travel *feel* real. You might describe the clothing you're wearing, how the house is decorated, the lingo that is being used, the cars being driven, music played, political landscape... there's so much to pick from, so have fun choosing what you want to use. It will bring your story to life and weave in new dimensions for your Mind Movie.

I tell a story called "Cheese Soufflé" in my personal storytelling work.

"It's 1971. I'm six years old and sitting at the kitchen table with my dad and two sisters. We're nervous. My mother is standing next to the olive-green refrigerator, tapping her hands on the orange Formica counter. She bends down to stare into the matching olive-green oven to watch her masterpiece, a cheese soufflé, come to life."

If you've got a story that starts far back in time, then stating the decade is helpful. Each decade comes with its own collection of instant mental images for the listener because each decade has some style and political, historical, or even personal connotations. Let's walk through a few of them to give you an idea of how the elements of each decade can be woven into your stories when applicable. These examples are more American-based, so if that's not your home country or culture, you can still investigate the evolution of your culture by decade

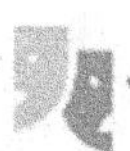

to pick out the era's details to help paint your own pictures accordingly. It's a fun exercise and worth putting into your Story Library as a reference while you craft your pertinent stories.

ERAS ARE REPLETE WITH GEMS TO ADD TO YOUR MIND MOVIE.

1950s: Men wore suits, women were typically "homemakers." Teens were at burger joints playing the jukebox and sipping pop at malt stands. It was the *Leave It To Beaver* era and Rockwell paintings were being sold as the American Dream.

1960s: The early half of the decade was Jackie O and JFK. Dress was still somewhat conservative; then the Beatles brought rock-n-roll, and by the end of the decade, we saw Love Power and Flower Power with Sex, Drugs, and Rock-n-Roll taking hold.

1970s: The United States was fighting in Vietnam and Women's Rights were being pushed to higher levels of importance. Disco was hot and everyone was groovy. Homes were laced in Olive Greens and Orange Formica, with appliances to match. Mom started wearing pantsuits and Dad's ties were short and squat.

1980s: Bigger was better with shoulder pads, or if you preferred the ripped look, the movie, *Flash Dance*, brought us loose sweatshirts and leg warmers with *Candies* pumps. Many kids were "turnkey" as both parents were in the workforce, and the world watched Prince Charles marry Princess Diana.

1990s: Casual owned the runways, and Nirvana's avant-garde 'Grunge' sound was taking the music industry in a whole new direction. Unplugged guitars, huge cell phones, and car phones were "classy." K-Pop took the music scene globally. The world mourned the death of Princess Diana.

2000s: We survived Y2K, but then the Internet tech boom bombed. We saw terrorism on US soil with 9/11; wealth plummeted, the housing bubble burst, and families battled these financial hits. Rap artists, musicians, and almost ANYONE were now becoming YouTube icons; mesh clothing and really expensive sneakers were the new status. Our iPod was our own pocket DJ.

2010s: Beyonce, Rhianna, and supermodels everywhere. Music is streamed everywhere. Black Lives Matter; Occupy Wallstreet; and we almost had our first woman president—and the country started to divide quickly. Talking politics at Thanksgiving dinner was not advised.

2020s: We opened with the Pandemic, turning our 3D lives into 2D zoom meetings; it became terrifying to even go to the grocery store or ride a bus; our political system has been attacked at every level; scientists, especially infectious disease or environmental, hold microphones and talk into cameras like never before. A Spiritual Awakening gets momentum.

Get the picture? Time travel happens in stories, and by pulling in era elements, your Mind Movie starts to thrive.

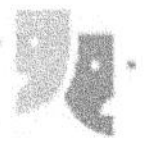

GEAR SHIFT SMOOTHLY INTO YOUR TIME TRAVEL

In some ways, I look at time travel like I'm driving a stick-shift car. I shift into one scene of time-space reality, and then as I move into the next-event sequence that is a memory (past tense), I say things that will make the shift smooth and not rickety. Let's revisit:

I'm standing in the company breakroom and my colleague, Megan, stands in front of the microwave, warming up some tea. "I've got to leave early today to bake brownies for my kid's theater's opening night."

Suddenly I'm sixteen years old. It's the 1980s and my best girlfriend is over for a slumber party. We've got our favorite soap opera, *General Hospital,* playing on our VCR and brownie batter in a huge bowl as we take out spoons to enjoy the dangerous, raw-egged batter. We're not going to get sick—this is the best part of the baking journey. None of us knew that raw egg was dangerous then.

BEEEEEP! The microwave bings— *and I snap back to my office breakroom. Where am I? Oh, right. I'm at work.* Megan darts out, "See you tomorrow!"

Using time travel in a story should be delicate, yet deliberate. Use carefully chosen words to let us know we're leaping time/space realities with you. If you aren't clear about whether you're moving backwards in time or forwards to the future, your listeners could get confused and start to **Wonder/Wander** from you.

Here's another example of time travel.

EDNA

It's a sunny day in Blue Earth, Minnesota when I visit the factory plant for the first time. It's buzzing in there, literally, from the machinery and the workers' detailed work. I see almost a hundred plant workers, mostly women, and one in particular catches my attention. I'll call her Edna.

Edna sits on a pillow to stop her back from aching. She's been sitting there for over twenty years, Monday to Friday. She has a large magnifying glass in front of her and wears protective eye goggles. She's holding a soldering iron as she meticulously solders a cable, like a surgeon working on an artery. I recognize the cable she's working on!

Suddenly I'm twenty-five years old, I'm working as an engineer in the navy on nuclear power ships. I'm standing on the *George Washington* in the Persian Gulf that hosts huge aircraft and about five thousand military men and women. We are in "harm's way" and safety is everything. The planes are huge, and inside them, I'm seeing cables that act as the central nervous system to keep the pilots on course and return them back to us.

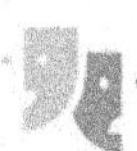

A loud buzzer from one of the plant machines draws me back to the factory floor in Minnesota. Edna is still soldering. Right then I realize that working for this company is deeply personal for me. That we have mission-critical responsibilities to see our troops' safety so that they come back home to their families as soon as possible. And now, I'm in Minnesota, ensuring that we do just that with Edna.

—CFO, Electronics Innovation Systems

TIME TRAVEL TRANSITIONAL PHRASES:

- "In an instant"
- "Instantly"
- "Suddenly I'm...."
- "My mind flashes back to...."

Weak and cliché Time Travel transitions:

- Fast forward
- Rewind to
- Cut to... (I heard this a lot in Los Angeles as a film pitch vernacular)
- To make a long story short..."

(Guess what? You just made a short story long.)

"I remember" is also not very powerful because it's a subtle way to jolt the listener out of your real-time Mind Movie and remind us that you're telling a story. It's not the end of the world if you say "I remember..." but I always try to coach my students to try other ways of slipping time travel into their stories more creatively.

THE POWER OF PRESENT TENSE

Notice in many of these stories, The Edna Story for example, we are in the present tense, not the past tense. **This is a magical storytelling move,** and those who master storytelling know that to tell the story in *present tense* is key. Why? Because when you are in the present tense, you are pulling the listener into the Mind Movie *with* you. The Edna Story present tense transports us onto the ship in real time and then back into the plant in real time. The scenes theatrically change, and we're walking on the floors that the teller is walking on. We're seeing what he is seeing. When you speak in the *past* tense, your listeners remain a little distant from the story, including the Storyteller. Your listener is outside of it, watching the story, but not fully emotionally engaged as they could be with you. This is a *tricky technique and* *takes intention and practice*, but it's so worth it. I personally felt my storytelling abilities were elevated when I learned the present-tense method.

Some of my storytelling friends have shared that it is also okay to move to past tense *during* a flashback. So, in the Edna story, as the Teller, you could change tenses. It's a personal choice as long as you are clear that you've moved to a flashback.

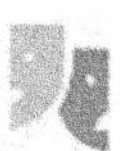

CHAPTER ELEVEN

WEED WHACKING

When a story is being born, you're going to ramble a bit, but I like to think of it as exploring. You're letting the Creative Flow move freely through you, sometimes feeling like your keyboard or pen is working for you, and you are simply the messenger. A perfect state for writing. As the memories bubble up, let them out. Savor them and allow the images to come to the surface as your words communicate the pictures you see, hear, smell, taste, touch, and reflect on. There is no wrong way to do this, other than stifle it too soon. As you repeat the story, you get to chisel it down. Or, as my storytelling friend, Kory May, likes to say, *"Take ten pounds of spinach and boil it down to that cup we need!"*

This is truly the fun part of storytelling, but also the hardest when you're new at it, because it means you *have* to choose between your best lines and words that keep the story train on the Mind Movie tracks and allow yourself to *let go* of the rest. You may use some scenes or sentences later, but for now, when you only have a finite amount of time to get your audience listening, you must edit, or what I call: **Weed Whacking.** We've been Weed Whacking when editing out characters, as well as time travel moments. It's a part of the creative process and it's important for your Mind Movie.

When I first started storytelling on a professional level, I struggled to edit scenes because I arrogantly (or novice-like) thought each one was brilliant and fun to play in, but really, they needed **Weed Whacking**. I have also found that some of the scenes that end up on the editing floor have reappeared in another scenario. So don't think that the time spent building that short story was wasted—it wanted to come out—and it will tell you when it's ready to be shared. **No time is wasted when your heart is telling a story.**

Editing things also brings the focus of your Mind Movie into clearer view. As you whack out weedy scenes that are just taking up space, you'll start to see the story arc bloom. And when I say "scenes," you'll learn in storyboarding that every story is made up of a series of scenes. Early drafts will flood out scenes and may even grow a few, before you know if you need anything whacked out. As we study more, you'll learn the **art of Weed Whacking.**

Below is an early draft from Crystal Clenney, CEO/Founder of INTUITVE HUMAN.

She really let every thought and image come out and plays with how to say something a few different ways. It's like she is "trying on" ways to say it and will feel which is best and cut the rest. I'll emphasize those moments where her Creative Flow is trying on different ways to say something the same way:

THE UNIVERSE'S WARNING
(DRAFT ONE)

It's 2004 and I'm twenty-seven years old, living in Grand Rapids, Michigan. I keep having these *crazy, repetitive, every night, every day dreams, visions, premonitions, signs* that I am going to die in a car accident. I feel it *in my bones, my tissues, my cells*—I feel it deeply—and it is too much. I am only twenty-seven years old. I think, *Really, Universe? This is how I'm going to die? A car accident? I mean, this is a lot to take in. I don't think I can process this!* I begrudgingly surrender. I must let it go. What else can I do?

Six months later, still dream-haunted, I decide to do something playful. I'm meeting a friend at Six Flags at 9:00 a.m. when the doors open. I can't wait for all that fun, riding rollercoasters all day! We're going to scream our heads off. I'm so excited and so *I'm getting up early, like 4:00 a.m. early… it's no big deal. I don't mind at all. I'm an early bird rooster. No problem, 4:30 a.m., I'll rise and shine with the best of them.*

It's 4:30 a.m. and the Michigan summer rainstorms *are pounding down on the roof of my car. I can't see the cars in front of me. There are sheets and sheets of rain just pouring down the windshield. I have my wipers on full throttle, but it doesn't matter because the rain's velocity is winning right now. Should I pull over and let it pass? Should I turn around?* I look at the clock and realize, "No. I'll be late for my 9:00 a.m. fun." As I'm white knuckling the steering wheel thinking, *You've got this, you can handle it,* there is suddenly a flash of what looks like a guy running in front of my car. *He comes out of nowhere. Why is there a guy in the road at this hour?*

"TURN RIGHT!" I hear my Gut Instinct say to me, and so I do—and I swerve into an oncoming truck. My car turns horizontal and slides across the freeway, heading perpendicular to a red truck. It's all happening really fast, and I spend the next ten seconds panicking.

I've crashed. I'm actually in a car accident. Holy smokes. I'm not dead though. Not even a scratch. I grab my umbrella and head towards the truck. The driver is pounding his hands on his steering wheel as he's clearly upset too. As I approach, I see another man on the ground in front of the truck's grill. *He's busted up really bad. His right arm is twisted and not in the shape any arm is supposed to be, that's for sure.* He's dressed in a mechanic's uniform and his name tag (changed his name for the story) says "Pete." *He's murmuring. I can't understand him.* I hold the umbrella over him and tell him, "We're getting help and you'll be okay!" *I don't know if that's the truth, but my Instinct says to calm him as a transition out like this is scary to the departing soul.* So, I do.

Sadly, Pete didn't make it. It was a devasting life event, which took on more stories, but it taught me that my dreams are my guide. The fact that it repeated so many times, to the point where I thought it was only me who would die, was in fact a warning that I'd be there and present for another soul who departs.

After that, the haunting dreams never returned. They were all a premonition.

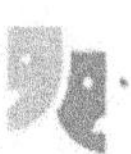

Crystal's story has suspense and high stakes right out of the gate, but her story was clocking in at nine minutes. I told her we needed to and could get it down to three. She didn't believe me. But guess what? We got it down to three minutes by choosing her words and scenes carefully. Below is the version where we whacked some weeds and streamlined her story for maximum impact.

THE UNIVERSE'S WARNING
(Draft Two)

It's 2004 and I'm twenty-seven years old, living in Grand Rapids, Michigan. I keep having a repetitive dream I am going to die in a car accident. I feel it in my bones. "Really, Universe? This is how I'm going to die, in a car accident?" I mean this is a lot to take in. I don't think I can process this!"

Six months later, I decide to do something playful. I'm meeting a friend at Six Flags at 9:00 a.m. when the doors open. I can't wait for all that fun, riding rollercoasters all day! We're going to scream our heads off in the name of fun!

It's 4:30 a.m. and the Michigan summer rainstorms are pounding down on the roof of my car. I can't see the cars in front of me. As I'm white knuckling the steering wheel, there is suddenly a flash of what looks like a guy running in front of my car. He comes out of nowhere. *Why is there a guy in the road at this hour?*

"TURN RIGHT!" I hear my Gut Instinct say to me, and so I do—and I swerve into an oncoming truck.

I've crashed. I'm actually in a car accident. Holy smokes. I'm not dead though. Not even a scratch. I grab my umbrella and head towards the truck. The driver is pounding his hands on his steering wheel as he's clearly upset too.

As I approach, I see another man on the ground in front of the truck's grill. He's busted up really bad. His right arm is twisted and not in the shape any arm is supposed to be, that's for sure. He's dressed in a mechanic's uniform. The name tag says "Pete." He's murmuring. I hold my umbrella over him and tell him, "We're getting help and you'll be okay!" I don't know if that's the truth, but my Gut Instinct said to calm him.

Sadly, Pete didn't make it. It was a devasting life event, but it taught me a lot, and that my dreams are my guide.

Your audience is smart, and they don't need it explained from every angle. They expect you to pick the best angle and just let them enjoy the ride. Don't overwhelm them. Give them the intellectual benefit of the doubt. Have fun with your free-flow creativity as it springs from

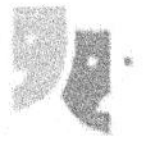

an oasis deep within you. Then take a step back and choose the words that resonate the most for you. **That's your Weed Whacker working.**

A PLUG FOR TIME CONSTRAINTS

For all the wonders of modern technology and all the good it does, our collective attention span has, unfortunately, shortened, thanks to the Internet. You're warned how much precious time you'll sacrifice with a three-minute read or thirty-second read. If you tell me it's a ten-minute read, it gets filed for "another time" when I think I have time for it. In fact, keeping your attention focused on something, allowing the idea to root itself in your mind, only takes seventeen seconds.

In business, I recommend that most of the stories you tell from your Story Library should range from **thirty seconds to three minutes maximum.** Personally, my favorite length is ninety-nine seconds. That's why rehearsing is key because the time constraint forces Weed Whacking. Telling stories within a limited timeframe is a very good exercise and goal as a Storyteller. You must choose your words wisely and not dilute them or derail your Mind Movie.

I've seen clients who had to give three-minute acceptance speeches, and as we rehearsed, they clocked in at 3:45 and wanted to beg to let that go. But, as they rehearse, they must Weed Whack, and when they give that time and concentration to it, they can make their time, and honor what was requested of them.

Time constraints boil a story down to its most pure essence. If you ever look at Netflix describe a series in just a few sentences, that's honoring time and space constraints. Play it. Edit. Weed Whack your words and your visuals and find the essence of your story and presentation. And then watch your audience's reaction to your succinct and thoughtful presentation. And guess what...because you're limiting how much data and info to go out, they will naturally spark questions. And when they ask questions, they are engaged, and that means your idea and thoughts are being heard. You're moving the train smoothly down the tracks to the Interest Station. Nice job, Storytelling Presenter!

GEOGRAPHY JUMPING

Like time-travel math, geography also does something funky to our brains. It makes us see maps, and if you're moving all over the map in your story, you're also all over the Mind Movie Map with your audience. Traveling that much can be mentally exhausting for the listener, so choose your location changes carefully. Or at least offer your listeners a bottle of water after having travelled that far with you!

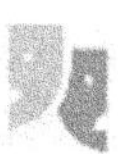

The best stories really limit locations. I've heard stories that took my breath away and they happened around the kitchen table. The Storyteller, Carolyn Erickson, was sharing flashbacks of her kids growing up, but the entire story scene was around that one spot: the family dinner table. It was beautifully told and had both personal storytelling value as well as business value.

If you had a powerful moment in the boardroom, then keep your story centered there as you describe and interact with the characters sitting around you. Each person is from some-where—what can you pull from their background that can help paint their personality more vividly, without jumping all over the map literally and figuratively?

An example:

As we gather around the boardroom, our CEO, a Texan who really missed his Stetson cowboy hat during these dry meetings, sits at the head of the table. To his right is our CFO, and she longs for the quiet days on the beaches of Maine, which I know from the pictures of her childhood home all over her office.

See? We're all still *in* the boardroom, but we are effortlessly jumping to other parts of the country to build character background so that we can better see and relate to them.

One example of a confusing way of handling geography jumping was when I watched a Storyteller give almost every physical move they had made while growing up. It was impossible to keep track of that many "Google Map red pins" in my head. I jumped off the story train somewhere between Southern California and Phoenix.

Editing your life to keep your stories crisp and easy to follow is absolutely on you as the Storyteller. Just like editing out characters that don't really move the story along, if you over-share all your life moves, you'll overwhelm and even bore your listeners. This type of mean-dering from place to place before you really get to the point of your story derails the train even before it leaves the station. So be objective about what's really relevant for your story, limiting the scene changes, the characters, and the events. We'll talk more about this in the chapter on Storyboarding—the weed whacking map to non-meandering.

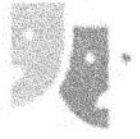

CHAPTER TWELVE

WOUND STORIES VS SCAR STORIES

When you are selecting your stories, it is always recommended that you sift through your life experiences and choose the stories that you can tell, and it doesn't sting anymore. Time has done its magic, and now when you recall that story, you're able to share the golden wisdom instead of the pain. Sharing like this can be healing to others. Those are Scar Stories. But if it hurts, or time has not had a chance to heal, then you're entering a Wound Story. Here's an example:

It's a rainy Friday evening in Seattle, Washington. Around three hundred people are gathered to listen to ten randomly selected storytellers come to the stage and share their five-to-six-minute *personal story* for "The Moth," the NPR Granddaddy storytelling show that reaches enthusiastic listeners all over the globe. The stakes of this show are competitive. There are three teams of randomly selected "judges" who will score your story from one to ten using decimals. So, you could get a 9.5 or a 6.0 on a story that you personally experienced. (These untrained strangers are essentially judging your storytelling and your life. No big deal.) The highest scoring story "wins" and moves onto a Moth Grand Slam.

Four storytellers had just finished their stories when a young man, probably in his mid-twenties, gets called up to the stage. He says, "I'm going to share a story about my father's death."

Okay, show us what you've got, I think.

He opens his story with "My father died on Wednesday...."

Gasps from the audience. Uneasy wiggling in their chairs. The entire audience realizes he is about to tell a massively huge wound story! His father passed away just *two days ago,* and he wants to share it with a room full of strangers on a stage?

You could hear the collective breath of the crowd draw in as we stare at this poor soul. *Don't do it, friend, don't do this now,* I think. *This is **not** an appropriate time to tell this story!* As the audience, we are there to learn and be entertained—not to be your grief counselor. Or perhaps someone may run up on that stage and hug you with a box of tissues in hand.

THAT IS A WOUND STORY.

He somehow managed to get through the five tremendously long minutes without breaking down, but it wasn't really fair to the audience. We were worried about him. And the next storytellers should not have been made responsible for redirecting the energy of the entire room and the remaining portion of the competition back to a place that comforts everyone at the competition. Telling emotionally sensitive stories publicly is something to avoid, unless it's a Celebration of Life or a funeral where time is not granted for healing. If you are asked to speak during such an event, you can use your storytelling skills to share memories of the recently departed much more vividly, yet tenderly for the grieving audience to absorb and appreciate.

I'm bringing this up as some of you may start to really enjoy the power of storytelling beyond the boardroom or office. The more you exercise your storytelling skills for business or personal storytelling venues, the better you will become. When you think about it, personal storytelling happens all day long —and mastery of anything means to not just study it, but to do it frequently, and eventually teach or coach it.

IF IT STILL HURTS A LOT TO TALK ABOUT, DON'T TELL IT YET.

They say time heals all wounds, so allow it to do its work before dragging your audience into something they may not want to hear yet. There's no need to drum up and feed those emotions and try to explain something you may still be trying to understand yourself. When trauma happens, it takes time to find the path of least resistance and head back towards happiness and ease. You may decide to never tell a story publicly if it hurts, and it's perhaps better done with your closest circle or a counselor who makes you feel safe.

In the business realm, we tend to naturally filter the super personal sharing out, and stick to subjects centered around our work and careers, but there are still many personal moments, like getting fired or laid off, parenting, owning a home, selling a home, sports stories and many more, in which you could find a metaphor for your work stories. But I suggest that you keep the wound stories out as they may not be good for you or your listeners.

If you are in a business, like Dr. Data, where your Life Science company is literally saving lives, then your core story, like "Meet Sarah," needs to be a fictionalized story, perhaps based on your experience, and communicates your *why* you do what you do to save lives. If you, however, share a personal story of someone who went to hell and back—wait until you can talk about it smoothly.

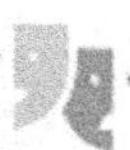

WHEN TO TELL A SCAR STORY

It's a 20/20 wisdom thing. If you can look back at a challenging or painful time, and you can see the rich lessons that it taught to you, and you can approach the story from that type of teaching perspective, then these are stories to add to your Story Library and are exactly why storytelling works so well. As shared countless times in this book, stories have the power to change the world. Just be selective on which stories you tell. We all want to see your journey of strength and resilience because it inspires others to think about their own paths. But *when* you tell it is an important decision that only you can make. If you have a "feeling" that it's too soon, then hold onto it. You may still be living through it, so allow it to unfold until you know the conclusion has been reached.

If that same broken-hearted young man whose dad passed away would want to share his scar story years later and share the healing moments he's had on his journey to enlightenment post-Dad, then that would be a great story to tell and hear. He might be stronger and wiser and have a story that can help others heal their own grief from a similar situation because he is no longer actively living it. He has perspective and wisdom to share and doesn't have an expectation that the audience is supposed to make him feel better about what's happened. He's taken responsibility for his story. And to an audience that wants to learn about the grieving process, this young man, due to time passing, could craft a beautiful talk around that death experience.

One of my own Scar Stories is about my personal challenge with Obsessive Compulsive Behavior (OCD) as a child and then as a parent. This story has been told on Ignite Seattle and a longer version with National Alliance of Mental Illness (NAMI), and it shares very personal and painful moments in my life as a child battling with my obsessive "swearing at God" types of thoughts, then terrified I would be struck down by lightening if I didn't wash my hands dozens and dozens of times a day.

Then watching it happen to my own kid felt horrible! I wanted to blame myself for "giving it to her via DNA," but by bravely crafting the story, I learned that I can influence those who battle OCD personally and give them hope. I can also educate those who don't understand the condition and get them to stop making insensitive statements using the Mind Movie technique.

UNINFORMED PERSON:	"Oh, my OCD is really showing today. Did you see how clean my desk is today?"
INFORMED PERSON:	"Oh, is this something you really deal with because I know OCD quite well. Are you getting help?"
UNINFORMED PERSON:	"Oh, I was just kidding."
INFORMED PERSON:	"Oh. Well, a person with OCD doesn't clean their desk because they *want* to, it's because they *have* to or something

bad is going to happen to themselves or someone they love. Can you imagine thinking a plane crashed, and it was because you didn't do your tapping ritual before washing your hands? Or having to check the oven and the lights twelve times before you can leave the house because if you don't someone will get hurt? It's really quite a mind prison."

NEWLY INFORMED: "Oh. I'm sorry for my insensitivity. I didn't realize and will not make an OCD joke ever again."

NOTE: If you want to see samples of Social Advocacy or Mental Health Stories, just go to my website and you'll see: "OCD IS A FAMILY AFFAIR" and also "WALKING THROUGH THE DOORS OF OCD" as well as, "Chocolate and Vanilla" a story about battling racism.

Visit: https://storyfruition.com/melissas-storytelling

CHAPTER THIRTEEN

USING DATA TO CREATE VISION STORIES

Before I started Story Fruition, I had been in media advertising sales most of my career, and specifically in advertising technology. We were pioneers taking on the Wild West of the Internet and seeing the potential of what computer and data science would bring to the world. And, like all startups, we had to tell Vision Stories and tell them *really* well to attract pioneer sponsors who would take that leap of faith.

The basis of this technology was data. How an online reader cruised a publisher's website; the articles they read mattered as we could glean the info to create virtual audiences that advertisers wanted to attract. And the technology gave the reader a more relevant experience as well because they were going to see an ad that matched their reading behaviors. Serve ads relevantly. This raw data when pooled together could create *personas* and then the story could be constructed.

This "new media" technology was revolutionizing our lives. And we had to paint the picture to the advertisers of how it worked and what it would mean for them. The stories we would tell were Vision Stories based on data.

Let's take some data sets and combine them to create a story for a fictional cruise line. Looking at the various indicators of the people who convert most, we see the following audiences rank highest. That's where the story structure and creativity begin in the data analysis and in the story building. For example:

- Gen X: Female
- Household Income: 125,000K-150,000
- Homeowner
- Kids at home / 8-12 years in age
- Sports enthusiast
- Business: Marketing
- Business: Domestic traveler
- Business: International traveler
- Restaurant lover
- Wine enthusiast
- Book lover: Fiction
- Health and Wellness enthusiast
- Geography: US

Total Audience: 1.4M

THE LOGICAL-LEANING STORY COULD BE:

Our technology has an algorithm that will classify user data sets to match affinities to unique users who are anonymized. This reduces the impression waste in order to deliver more relevant content to both the user and the advertiser. We refer to this as Behavioral Targeting.

Are you sitting on the edge of your seat from that explanation? Are you aching to write a check to support that vision? Maybe some people are if they see some graphs and charts to assist the analytical method. **The emotional version** of a Vision Story, however, is to identify "The Problem" with a relatable character, and then the technology is the hero in the story.

Meet Martha. She's forty-three and a mom to two tweens who love soccer. Martha is also a corporate marketing executive with a job that demands long hours and lots of travel. Her quest to be the working mom who still attends the soccer and football games for her sons has made Martha feel like she is stretched too thin and underserving her own personal needs. Missed yoga classes and take-out dinners are common because her work is pulling her away.

Martha would much rather spend that restaurant money on a vacation. She daydreams of resting on the Lido deck with a great novel, soaking up the sun as she makes her way around the gorgeous islands of New Zealand.

While Martha surfs the net, she notices a cruise ad in her newsfeed. It resonates with her. She clicks on it and hits the landing page. She volunteers some personal information because learning more about their cruises is fun—especially if they are about New Zealand.

Martha then jumps to a news site, where she sees the cruise line ad again. (This is called "retargeting.") This time the ad is about New Zealand ("dynamic creative"). A couple of days later, Martha gets a text sharing that the New Zealand trips are 30 percent off if you book by the end of the week ("Cross Device targeting"). Still tempting, but she's too busy with too many obligations to let that dream come to life just yet.

As Martha's days push on, she sees a video pre-roll while playing on YouTube about, you guessed it, New Zealand cruise vacations. "Okay, that's enough…I've got to go for it," she says. She pulls out her credit card and books her trip. (That's called a "conversion.")

So, dear advertiser, can you see how your ad dollars would no longer just be spent without any knowledge on what the return is going to be? Can you see how your relationship to Martha is dramatically improved, faster than traditional offline media methods? This is the power of digital media and why we're here with you today- to escort you to more effective and lucrative ways to invest your marketing money and see a higher return on that investment.

THE SEE SUITE

Sales and marketing executives are not the only ones to use Vision Stories to move the proverbial needle. Obviously, the entire C-suite needs powerful storytelling skills to set the tone of the company's mission and swoon investors. HR executives also need the power to provide vision to candidates, as well as employees that are about to be let go. **Vision Stories excite and comfort all at once.** They are the moment the human mind moves from the current state of affairs to the new tomorrow, sooner than anyone expects.

We will explore Story Library building later in this book, but you can see that a variety of stories based on data need attention and to be *humanized*. I see a lot of companies that haven't inserted any stories into their sales of presentation decks and that's a swing and a miss. Like Dr. Data, your messaging must be balanced with both relatable narratives and the science of business analytics. Remember, our brains thrive on story plus data.

Storytelling as part of the company culture will differentiate you and take you to the success you have been dreaming of and preparing for so embrace these stories. When I was growing up in Corporate America, the Case *Stories*, not Case *Studies* are what moved the needle. They still do!

RECAP PROCESS TWO: STORY CRAFTING

1. Use a simple story arc formula to create flowing stories that don't meander. This story arc also helps you keep control of your Advance and Expand moments.
2. C.R.O.W. allows us to be introduced to each character; understand their relationships; feel the stakes of the story; as we visually see where you are physically, mentally, and spiritually in life during the time of this story.
3. Senses: We must be able to see, hear, smell, taste, touch to *feel* your story.
4. Avoid the Wonder/Wander: As the presenter/storyteller, it's your obligation to keep the communication train on the tracks so be careful with your word choices, images, corporate speak, and anything that could confuse a listener.
5. Be deliberately clear when you are time traveling and geography jumping.
6. Weed Whacking is a fun way to approach editing. What's blocking us from seeing the garden when you have so many words or overused phrases that just need to go?
7. Crush your story with potent closing that ties your story back to valuable insights and takeaways for your audience.
8. Share stories when you are ready to tell them. Find the gold and share it with the world when you are ready and able to use storytelling for social advocacy.

STORYBOARDING

THE MAP TO YOUR MIND MOVIE

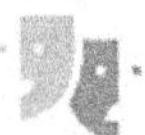

CHAPTER FOURTEEN

STORYBOARDING THE MAP TO YOUR MIND MOVIE

As I've been teasing along the way, a wonderful way to keep your Story Arc flowing is with Storyboarding. Award-winning storyteller and author, Matthew Dicks, shared this fabulous method at one of his Seattle workshops, and it is now fundamental to my own work. In fact, I rarely write a full script because the improviser in me encourages free-flow energy. And now you want to take your baby story and start to identify the "scenes" as your story unfolds.

Where does the story start? In a boardroom or on the factory floor? Who joins you in this story? A new character usually comes in during a new scene. As your story unfolds, more scenes are created that will bullet point some of the main points. You can also break your narrative and put them into the scenes, so it has a "script-like" feel for you to lightly memorize easier.

My executives appreciate storyboarding because they've learned it saves time and is much more freeing. When we move into written scripts, we are putting pressure on the Storyteller to worry about memorization, and this is NOT an actor's monologue of another playwriter's words. It's different.

Storyboarding is similar to the bullet points of a PowerPoint presentation and feels more comfortable than reading the script under the slides. When a presenter reads their scripts, their authenticity wanes, and the audience's engagement drops because if you are too busy to learn your stories off-script, then why should they invest their full attention in listening to you? Let alone their money. It makes the presenter seem unprepared when they decide "I'll just wing it." I'm not saying that having notes at a podium isn't helpful, but don't use them as a crutch. Lift your head and look at your audience. Connect with them during the story portion of the talk. You will do so confidently when you've rehearsed each Mind Movie scene, and your own imagination may even be able to see the storyboard to keep you on track.

One of my favorite leadership clients is Denise Cooper from North Carolina. She has been a Human Resources executive, author, keynote speaker, and Leadership Coach to many powerful CEOs, and helps them solve problems that many thought were impossible. Denise does not hear "No" or "That can't be done." Her creative dedication and excitement when solving a problem is impressive. As such, during our work together, finding stories was *not* a problem for Denise, but like so many of my clients, it's *how* to piece the story together scene-by-scene that's the real challenge. What to keep? What to dump? What to condense? When to Weed Whack to make the story more interesting and concise without meandering? And, now add dialogue deliberately; okay, but where?

This is a Storyboard. Here's where the Storyteller plots their Mind Movie scene-by-scene. We apply C.R.O.W., senses, and even title each scene so that the Storyteller can mentally see where their story is headed as we move to the Aha! Moment, and then to the powerful reflection. Most stories land around seven scenes, but sometimes they are shorter.

SCENE TITLES

In Storyboards, you want to plot the order of your scenes, and to title them, which can help you remember the content. Each scene box is a tiny story, and your storyboard holds the key point to hit. The storyboard is a record of your story when you find yourself needing it later in time. And many times, a "scene" in one story may make it as its *own* story in an interview or conversation. Storyboards are tremendously valuable and what fill your Story Library.

Storyboard

SCENE 1   Scene Title:

SCENE 2

SCENE 3

SCENE 4

SCENE 5

SCENE 6

SCENE 7

www.StoryFruition.com

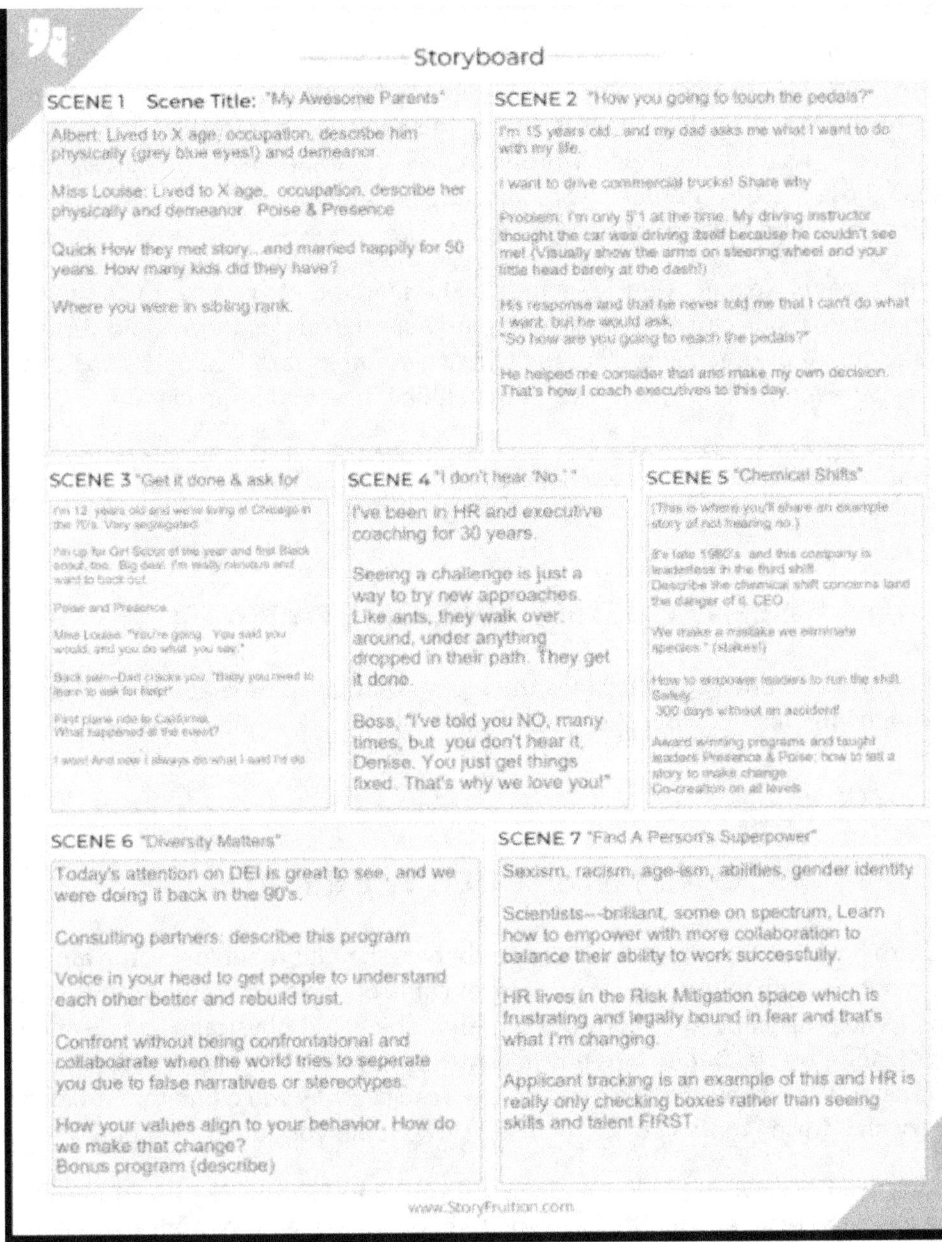

In Denise's storyboard, watch how we loop back and pull elements from scene one into subsequent scenes. Each scene is a smaller story in itself. When Denise is in a podcast interview as either the host or guest, she has a library of stories that she can pull from. She then lands with the leadership reflection that ties back to her book. What's marvelous about Denise is that she understands that *the written story*- because she is an accomplished author- is not exactly the same as *the oratory version*. What works written down has a whole other life when it's just her voice and a microphone.

Like many Story Fruitions, we find that childhood holds the early germinating moments that reveal the future leader. I always look at family upbringings and influences, both positive and negative, because both formulate who you are today. One is nurturing and teaches you love; the other contrasting side is teaching you perseverance, resilience, and your problem-solving skills. As a leader, being a problem solver is imperative and serves your higher purpose. So those "testing moments" are absolute gifts to you as you unfold and evolve as a leader when you share these pearls of wisdom.

In the first scene, we meet Denise's parents. She shared that growing up on the south side of Chicago in the 1960s came with extreme, in-your-face segregation and a reputation for drugs, crime, and broken families. *"But my family was happy and loving. We had a great life. My parents were fantastic,"* says Denise, with genuine, heartfelt appreciation.

As we move through her storyboard, we then prove this with moments with each parent who taught her basic life lessons that sculpted her leadership abilities later in her career.

SCENE ONE: MY AWESOME PARENTS:

We meet Denise's parents. She describes them physically and a little about their relationship and growing up in Chicago. How she feels about them and how they treat her. All following C.R.O.W.

SCENE TWO: TOUCH THE PEDALS?

We start with how Dad taught her to never doubt herself or let roadblocks stop ambition. But when her young dream to become a truck driver came up, he simply and gently asked logical questions to help his baby girl figure out whether she could physically handle the requirements of driving a big rig. Denise was tiny in stature, under the 5'0" mark. When he heard her dream, he said, "Well, baby, that's a great career. I can see why you'd find that exciting, seeing the country and driving that big truck. (Pause.) How would you touch the pedals, honey?"

He didn't tell her, "You can't do that because you're too short." No, he let her figure that out using logic and respect, and Denise came to her own conclusions and course corrected.

That one moment in Denise's life resonated all the way to her core, so as a leader in Human Resources, she applies the same logic. Instead of telling people what to do, she acts like a *Leadership Sherpa* to help them draw their own realizations. Strong leaders know that respecting people for their talents is far more empowering than dictating and shaming creativity. This story we call "Touch the Pedals" can exemplify that lesson in any moment Denise needs to illustrate that point to another leader.

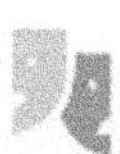

SCENE THREE: GET IT DONE!

We meet her beloved and wise mother, Ms. Louise, who knew that Denise must always do two things:

1. Do as you said you would do. "Get it done. Get it done! Get it DONE."
2. Do it with "Poise and Presence."

The Girl Scout story demonstrates her mother's dedication to this premise. It was vital to Denise's mother that her daughter learn to walk elegantly with a pile of books on her head and enough presence to own any room she entered. So, at 5'1", many people think Denise is actually six inches taller simply because of the poise she holds. She emanates that aura when walking into any room, and this started at the age of twelve when she was taught to, "Hold your head high, eyes focused straight ahead, connect to your audience."

SCENE FOUR: I DON'T HEAR 'NO':

We now time travel from precious childhood lessons to being an adult and making her way in her career. But the two stories: "Touch the Pedals" and "Poise and Presence" are now threading into her larger story. Her boss says, "Denise doesn't hear no," and she responds with, "That's not true!" and he respectfully says, "Denise, I've told you NO many times, but you just keep coming back with problem-solving solutions. You just get things done."

SCENE FIVE: CHEMICAL SHIFTS

This is a HUGE and fantastic story/scene for Denise. She has told it and landed six-figure deals from sharing it to highlight her leadership style, so she tells it frequently. Often, when creating your storyboard for your core Story Fruition, you'll need to expand to more storyboards, which we did. That's the fun of finding and crafting your own core Story Fruition: you will find a variety of mini stories that you can pull from as needed.

SCENES SIX AND SEVEN: CORE POINT AND REFLECTIONS

The last two boxes of the storyboard are usually about tying everything you've shared up in a neat bow to remind your audience why you shared any of these stories in the first place. You are sharing what you've learned, why it changed you, and *how* it changed you, and possibly even your organization. This is where your Sage steps up and into your storytelling, so enjoy it, because your unique perspective and viewpoint are your legacy.

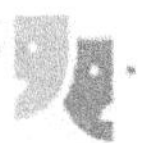

THE STORYBOARDING AND WEED WHACKING PROCESS

This is your map of your story of transformation. As you revise your storyboard, the imperative scenes and moments stay; a flurry of words become carefully selected words; vague images become vivid; pauses find their place; and the emotional delivery drives the entire story home. This is the perfect time for your *own* **Gut Instinct** to guide you on what stays, what grows, and what gets tossed aside.

> *Storyboarding stops the meandering problem most people have because it provides the map from beginning, middle, and end.*

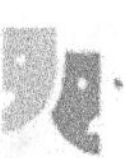

RECAP PROCESS THREE: STORYBOARDING

1. Storyboarding helps you memorize your presentation or story scene-by-scene.
2. Storyboarding acts as a record of the story to refresh you or teach new people the story.
3. Play in each scene as you rehearse to find the golden nuggets of emotional impact.
4. Show us the characters talking to us scene-by-scene so that your story comes alive to us.
5. Conclude with your reflections and tie up why this story has a business purpose.

SIMPLIFYING YOUR PRESENTATION SLIDES

CHAPTER FIFTEEN

CRAFTING YOUR INVESTOR
OR SALES PRESENTATIONS TO TELL YOUR STORY

I've seen thousands of investor and sales presentations in my career, and most of them, at first viewing, are crowded, confusing, and have the kitchen sink thrown in. The deck looks like it is panicking to cover all the information they have ever uncovered in their journey, which is just not true, necessary, or desired. This chapter will focus on investor decks, but the same principles apply to any sales, board meeting, or partner presentation. Keep the slides simple, not crowded.

Your presentation, especially your first round with an investor or partner, needs to be of a higher level and **simple**. Its goal is simply to get the listener to understand and nod their heads that you've got an idea possibly worth funding and getting them to a "yes." Courting an investor is like dating. It takes time to share information. The more interest they have in your idea, the more you reveal. You don't need to reinvent the wheel. You are going to change the world, so don't complicate it!

And please do not bore or confuse them.

So, let us approach the deck with a Weed Whacking mindset, and make sure it is supporting you as the presenter, not upstaging you. I usually know whether my services are needed by the first slide. Why? The presenter opens with unemotional stats and graphs, thinking that is going to charge the room up right away.

DATA FIRST VS STORY FIRST

I had the pleasure of meeting the CEO of a start-up out of South Korea, Mr. Jung Suh. He is an interesting man whose noble mission is to help restaurant owners remain in business and thrive. Most owners do not study the science behind running a successful restaurant, so the reality is that four out of five restaurant owners will close their doors in less than five years. That's a sad figure if you think about it. Restaurants are a joyful human experience and contribute greatly to our communities through food, conversation, and connection. Keeping a restaurant thriving keeps our neighborhoods thriving when you think about it. We want them to flourish.

When we first met, he was excited to embrace a new way of presenting his idea using storytelling. I love it when people immediately feel that this reapproach can be expansive for their success and confidence. So, we got to work. His first opening slide, like most decks, opened with lots of graphs and data:

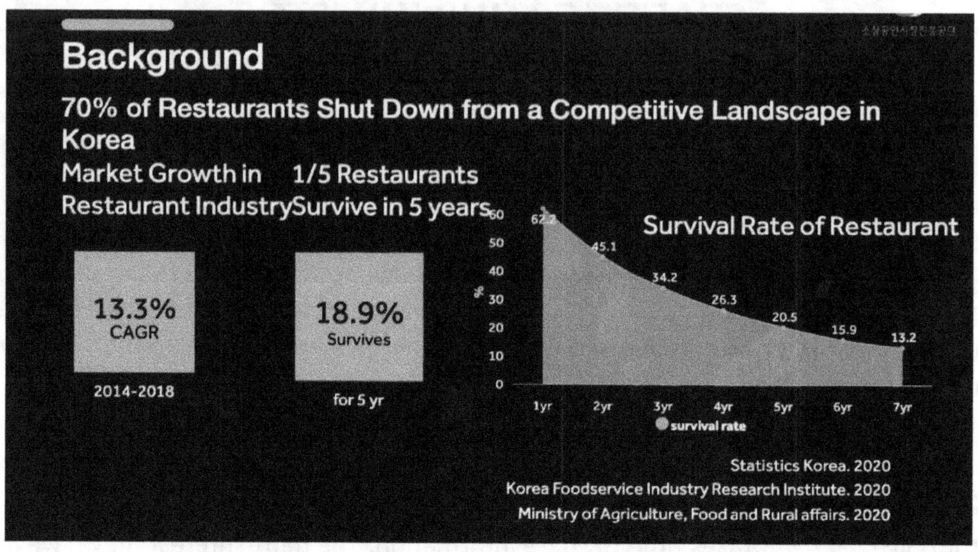

When a presenter opens with this many data, stats, graphs, and footnotes right out of the gate, they overwhelm the listener. A person cannot effectively read this graph and listen to the presenter at the same time. So, there goes the train off the track—and the struggle to regain interest is at stake. Their story, however, is about helping restaurant owners use data to make smart decisions—and like I've said throughout this book, no graph can create the emotional impact we need—but the story does.

What we did was we used the data within the narrative to connect them effectively together. We created a restaurant owner that typically falls into the "four out of five" and used pictures to help paint the "problem" for more emotional impact. Here's the script we created:

Meet Kim. She has always dreamed of owning her own café. It's an exciting lifestyle and she has all the enthusiasm to make it a tremendous success! She imagines happy customers regularly coming in to enjoy all her original dishes and fresh food.

The reality of running a successful restaurant, however, is not so exciting. Kim is going to be one of the four out of five restaurant owners to close after just five years. Why is this statistic so high? Because most restaurant owners do not understand the science behind the counter. The cost of food, the traffic of their customers, and the demand for particular dishes on certain days are hazy. Restaurant owners like Kim are making important decisions based on impulse or guessing, and not on real-time data facts. You need both to be successful long term.

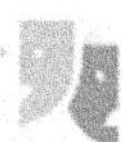

Kim is on the road to failure, her childhood dream and income shattered, and she doesn't even know it.

INFUSE THE DATA INTO YOUR STORY

According to highly successful Korean restauranteurs, the sweet spot for the cost of food per plate should be at 38 percent because that leaves enough room to handle the additional overhead that is required to run the business. Sadly, it has been uncovered that due to the lack of real data knowledge, most restaurant owners are paying almost 50 percent in food costs for their ingredients, which reduces their ability to keep operations in line.

It does not have to be that way.

HERO/PROBLEM SOLVER

Enter Sicpama where we provide Kim and others like her with the ability to know the facts behind various data sources so that she can make smart, reasonable, and profitable decisions that feed her customers, pay her employees and keep the lights on!

Using our software and Artificial Intelligence, Kim's sales are tracked so she knows when to prepare for customer surges and dish demands. This vital data allows Kim to be staffed accordingly, as well as making sure she orders the right amount of ingredients to meet popular menu demands on those specific days. No one wants to "86" a popular item as that can frustrate customers and ultimately be bad for business.

—Jung Suh, CEO, Sicpama AI, S. Korea

We'll stop here and look closer at what the story intends to achieve: emotional buy-in. The presentation is then shown with lovely pictures of Kim's dream and sets up Sicpama as the hero to save the day! Interest mounts because a good story builds up for the climax—and in this business story, we still need to see how the software works as the presentation moves into more data like Go-To Market Strategies, Competition Graphs, and Growth Projections, Traction and Team—but it all plays cohesively in telling the Sicpama story overall. Each slide is a story in itself—not just data being spewed at the listener.

This presentation was completed in just 99 seconds, or 350 words concisely, adding the human connection with relatable characters. This approach of using a small story to show "The Problem" is what people will remember. A good pitch presentation will make us care about the problem and invest in your solution. This also helps build trust that your team is the right team to get it done. All three elements matter. None can be missed.

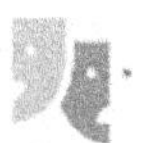

Next, we added the pictures. Let's look at how we adjusted his opening now using slides as support visuals to hold attention and build interest out of the gate. This is just the opening of the presentation we built together, highlighting the narrative. His complete presentation included a nice balance of graphs only when necessary to keep the communication train on the tracks—to only show what someone needs to know, not show everything.

PROBLEM:

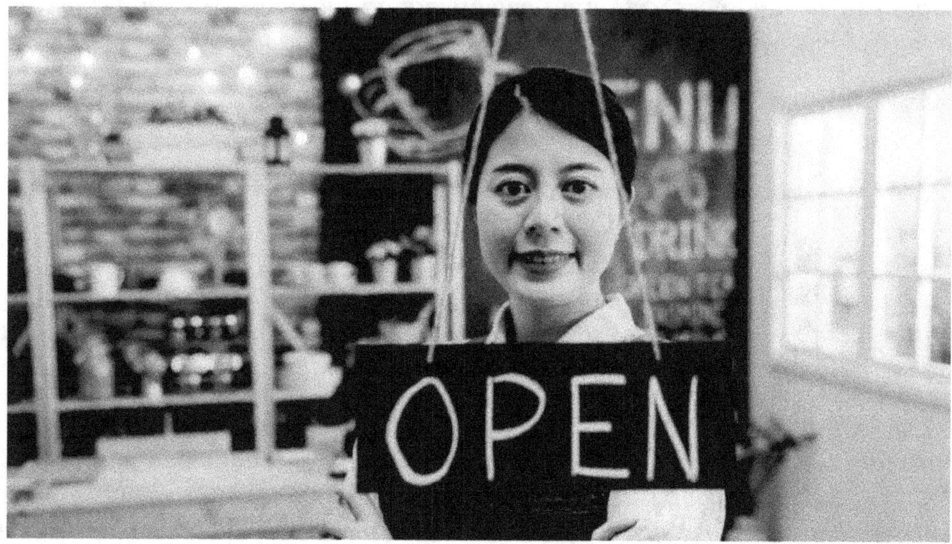

Meet Kim. She has always dreamed of owning her own restaurant café. It's an exciting lifestyle and she has all the enthusiasm to make it a huge success!

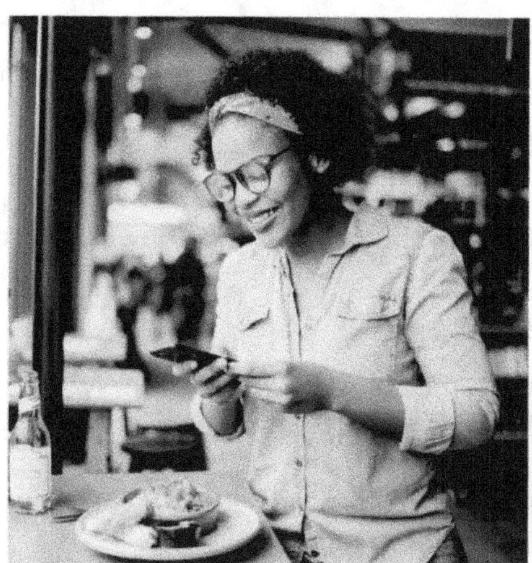
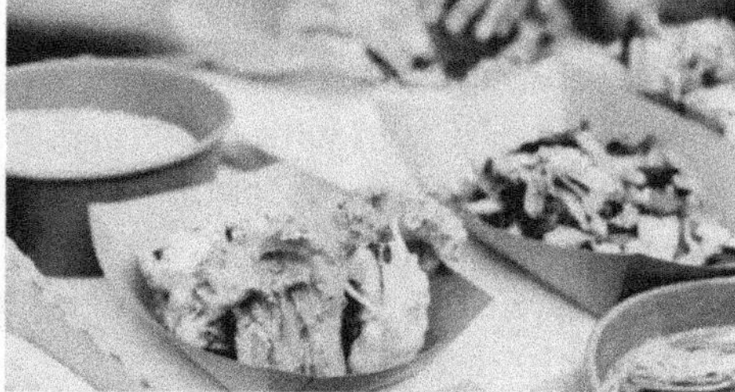
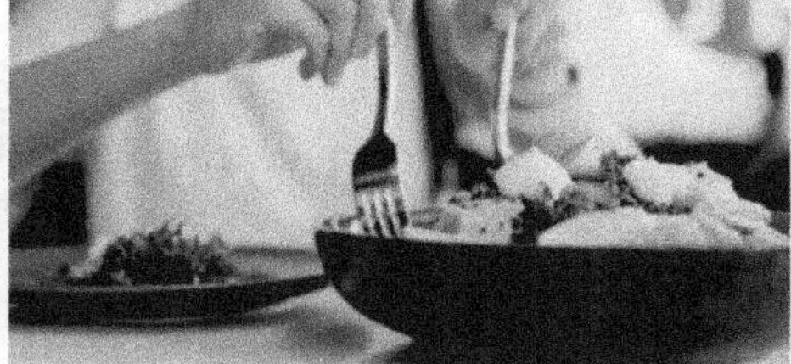

She imagines happy customers regularly coming in to enjoy all her original dishes and fresh food.

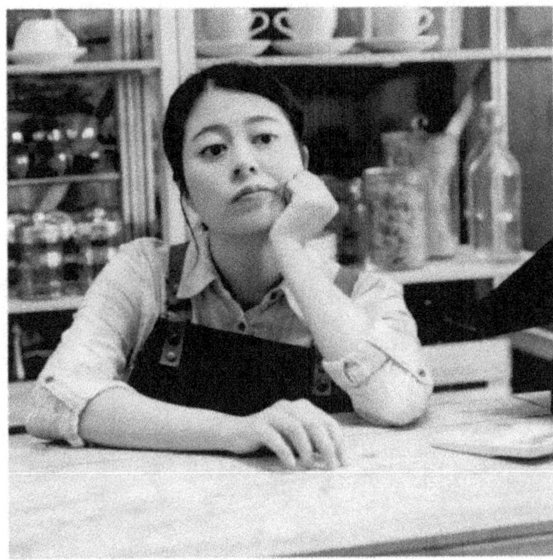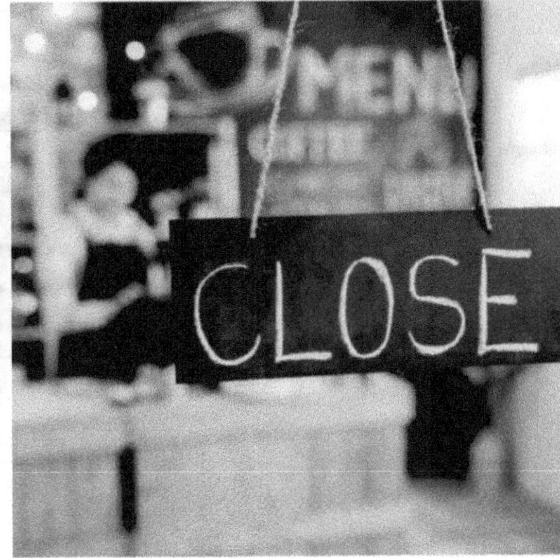

The reality of running a successful restaurant, however, is not so exciting. Kim is most likely going to be one of the four out of five restaurant owners who close down after just five years. Why is that so high? Because most restaurant owners do not understand *the science behind the counter*. The cost of food, the traffic of their customers, the demand of particular dishes on certain days is hazy. Restaurant owners like Kim are making important decisions based on gut instinct, not on data facts. You need both kinds to be successful.

According to highly successful Korean restauranteurs, the sweet spot for the cost of food per plate should be at 38 percent because that leaves enough room to handle the additional overheads that are required to run their businesses. Sadly, it's been uncovered that due to a lack of real data knowledge, most restaurant owners are paying almost 50 percent in food costs for their ingredients, which reduces their ability to keep operations in line.

SOLUTION:

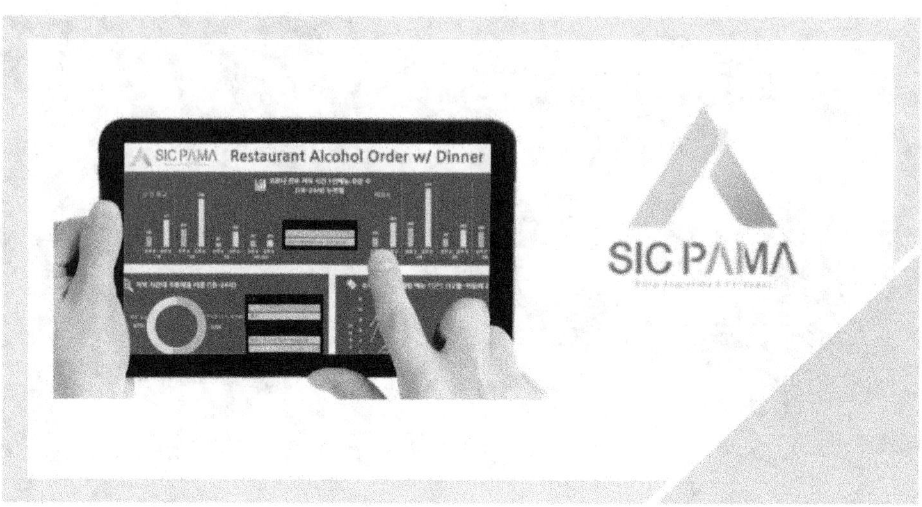

It doesn't have to be that way.

Enter SicPama. We provide Kim and others like her with the facts behind the various data sources so that she can make smart, reasonable, and profitable decisions that feed her customers, pay her employees, and keep the lights on!

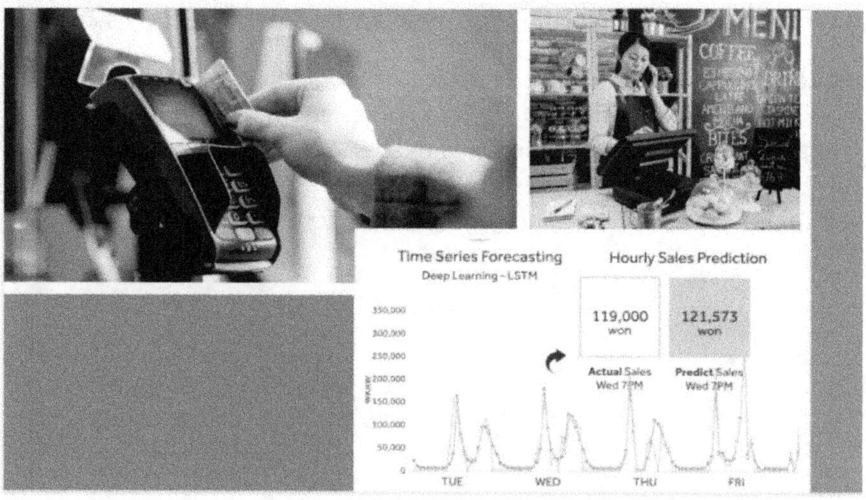

Kim's sales are tracked so that she understands when to prepare for customer surges so that she's staffed accordingly, as well as able to order the necessary ingredients so that her bestsellers are ready to be delivered to her customers.

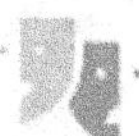

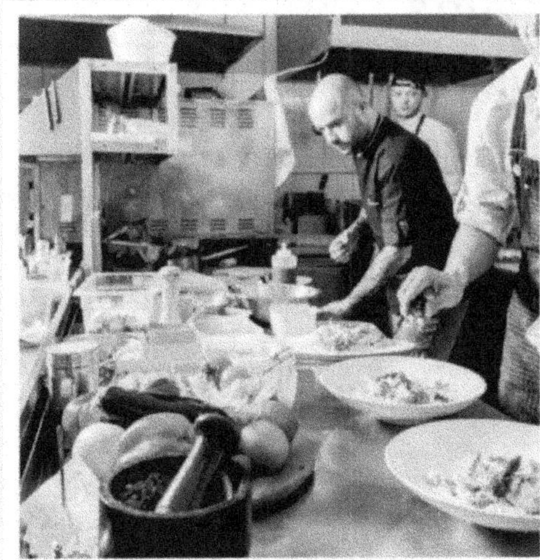
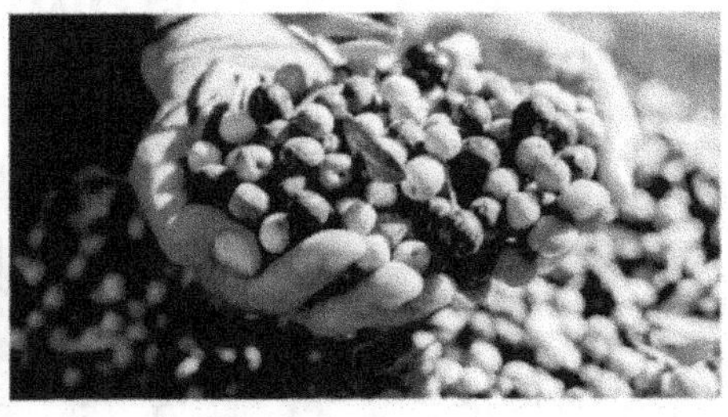
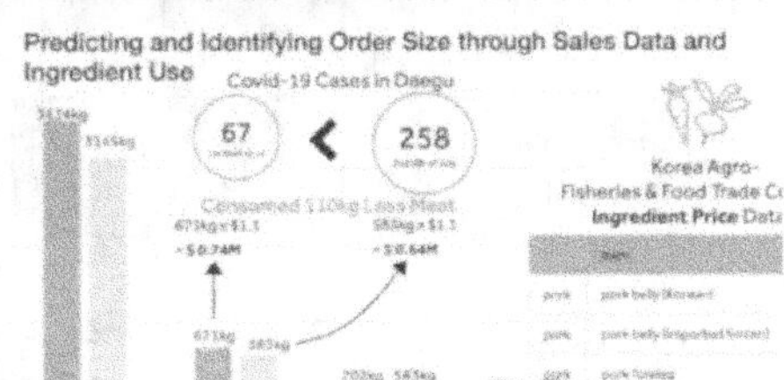

Now Kim knows what ingredients she needs to buy as well as the recommended quantities based on last week's traffic and sales patterns.

Do you see how the blending of images and data *into* the narrative of their problem/solution keeps the pitch moving forward and easier to understand? Sometimes we only used an image, and sometimes we highlighted data more dominantly. All of it blended to tell an emotionally compelling story to lead investors to say 'yes.'

HOW TO DERAIL YOUR COMMUNICATION TRAIN

I tell my clients to remember that your *oratory presentation* slides need to be designed differently from your *leave behind slides*. When someone is listening to you present, your job is to keep their attention and make sure they understand what you are trying to say. As I put it (several times by now), as the Storyteller, you are responsible for keeping the train on the tracks. Every time, EVERY TIME, you put a crowded slide up, you are essentially asking the listener to drop their active listening, lose their focus on you, and become a reader too. When your slide is confusing and wordy, *you* have derailed the train.

Many people read fast and try to beat the speaker; or some read more slowly, and the slide has moved on before they have fully absorbed all the information. Then what happens? Inside their heads, they might be thinking, *What was that slide trying to tell me? I only understood one-third of it because they moved on. Now I don't know where they are in this pitch. Okay, now I'm confused...and out.* When that happens, you only have yourself to take responsibility. They are now, you guessed it, in **Wonder/Wander**. Buh-bye!

So, let's look at more slide examples that take the train off the tracks in an *oratory* presentation.

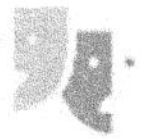

FLOW CHARTS

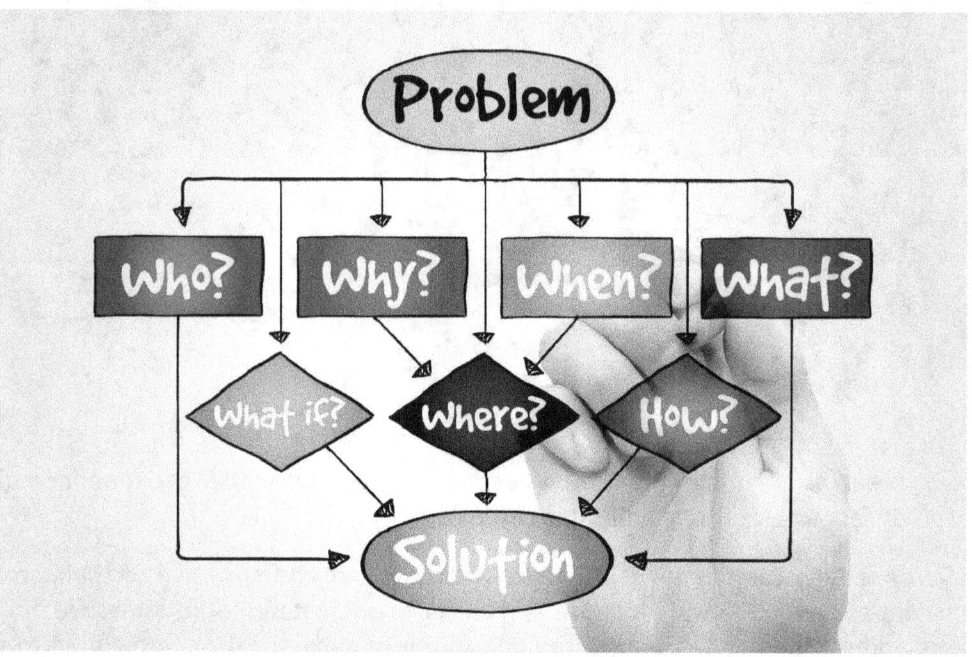

Let's talk about Flow charts. They are supposedly crowd-pleasers, but are they? Could you follow this slide easily while a speaker is talking? In a verbal presentation, the train falls off the tracks due to the lack of time to properly absorb and digest all the data. The neocortex is analyzing all the words, boxes and flow while the speaker is still talking. People can't do both successfully.

However, if this slide is *a leave-behind* slide that someone can take their time to read, then it could be fine to use. It's like a book: If the reader drifts off while reading, they can consciously become aware that they zoned out and easily go back and re-read the page on their time. But with oral presentations, the audience is not in control of when the slide is going to change—and when it's busy, some people will not finish understanding the content before the speaker changes the slide. The listener has fallen off the track and the speaker loses their audience's connection. A good sign for a speaker to take note of is when you see phones out and being scrolled as they check out. I've seen this happen countless times before I started Story Fruition. In fact, as a former enterprise seller, I actually did it to clients too! We all did. So, let's work to improve this in our business communities and meetings.

I challenge you now to look at your presentation decks. Are you throwing in the kitchen sink with overwhelming amounts of data and charts? Do you have lots of long sentences that you expect people to read, or worse, you plan to read to them? The goal is to captivate the audience so that they lean in and actively pay attention to you and your idea. Your deck can make or break it—or, at the very least, slow the interest train down.

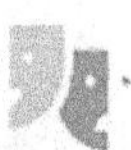

> *Stay in control of your story, your visuals and the balance of story to data, and you then become one of the most powerful people in the world, like Steve Jobs said! Go forth storyteller.*

Let's look at another example of a well-balanced data-to-narrative pitch.

"DOORS SHUT, DOORS OPEN!" LALO'S NINETY-NINE-SECOND PATH TO FUNDING

Juan Medina is the Founder/CEO of Lalo, an app that allows people to organize and keep memories of themselves or loved ones, so that after they depart this earth, they have a place to live on. When Juan first came to me for Founders Live Seattle, his presentation, like most of the presentations I see during the first round, was very technical and dry. His funding efforts were not headed in the direction he was after either. Every meeting ended with a, "Maybe later when you are more seasoned. This is too early for me right now." He was getting frustrated but not discouraged. He opened up and decided to re-think his strategy.

As I watched his initial pitch, I asked him about the name of his company. I love to learn how someone chooses their brand name.

"Lalo was my dad's name," he replied.

I asked more about his father and their relationship. It had been eighteen years since Lalo had lost his battle with Multiple Sclerosis. Juan was only twenty-four years old. There's never an easy time to lose a parent, but as a young man, that's a difficult time in your life to lose your number one male role model. He knew that his dad would not meet his wife or see his grandkids. While visiting his gravesite, Juan's wife asked him to share a story about his father, and Juan said, "I had nothing. When we lost my dad, we lost his family stories, his *empanada* recipes, and his bad dad jokes." That was Juan's *Aha Moment*. Many people like him were probably wishing they had a better way of holding onto those memories. He discovered that *fifty million people a year*, just in the US alone, lose someone they love. *What if he could help keep their memories alive?*

I could really relate to Juan. My parents had a huge influence on my life, and I was their caregiver for the last eight to ten years of their lives, and all I have left are some photos on my Facebook page, or as Juan pointed out, pictures in boxes or plastic bags. Their family stories, hearing them laugh, the family videos, are not easy to find. The Lalo app can correct that for all of us.

"Juan, why are you not sharing that story in your presentation since it's the impetus to you dedicating your life to building this app?"

He stopped and stared at me. I could see him processing my very simple question. "Because would anyone really care to hear it?" he asked.

JUAN'S WILLINGNESS TO SHOW VULNERABILITY CONNECTS US TO HIM

Juan's story is touching and packed with his heart. And, as the CEO of this start-up, he's essentially selling Storytelling, so by *not* sharing his story, he was only presenting the tech's nuts and bolts. Just like Dr. Data, it was a swing and a miss. His potential investors were not emotionally connecting to his pitch, and Juan was getting turned away.

Then Juan pivoted during our Founders Live time together. As a leader, the willingness to re-assess the current strategy and use data to make new decisions was put into action. So, we composed Juan's Lalo story.

"I think we should start your story right at your father's gravesite. That will instantly pull the listeners into a very vivid Mind Movie scene. They can't help but stand right next to you in that cemetery."

So, we did, and this is how Juan took his ninety-nine-second pitch and put balance back into his investor pitch.

Juan then converted his Founders Live presentation to an MP4 video and added music playing lightly in the background. Juan plays guitar, so it was a very personal touch, but you can get royalty-free music from a variety of places like Sound Cloud and YouTube. (Just credit the artist at the end of your deck.)

As we look closer at his pitch, how many powerful and beautiful images did Lalo weave into less than 250 words? Below are Mind Movie *images* that Juan created in the listeners' mind with very few images. In his presentation, he carefully controlled how much (or how little) was on each slide to keep the train on the tracks. His previous deck, which had a lot of data and kitchen-sink-looking slides, now moved to carefully and thoughtfully curated images that simply backed up and supported his storytelling rather than usurping his presentation control.

Here's Juan Medina's ninety-nine-second pitch.

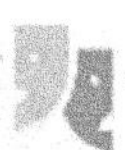

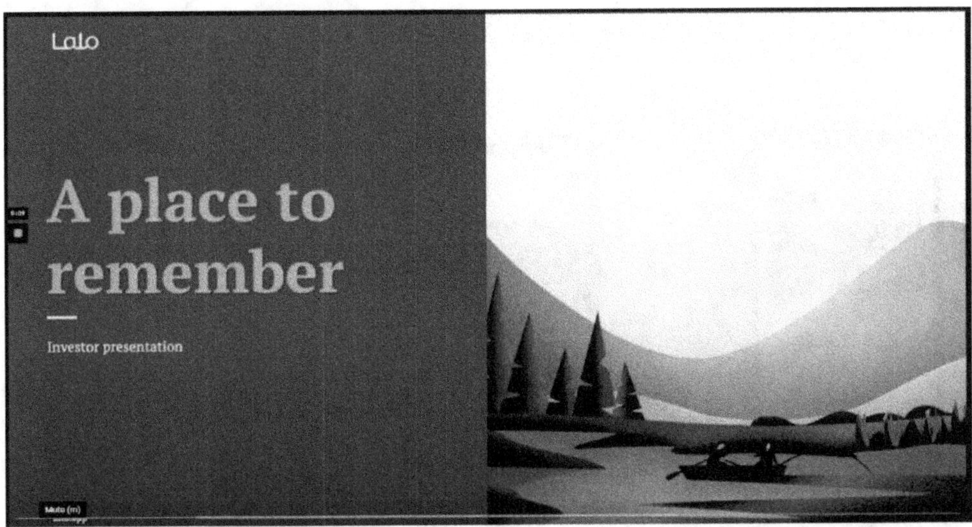

It's eighteen years after my father's death and *I'm standing at his grave with my family. My wife turns to me and says, "Juan, tell us a story about your dad!"* (pause) But I've got *nothing*.

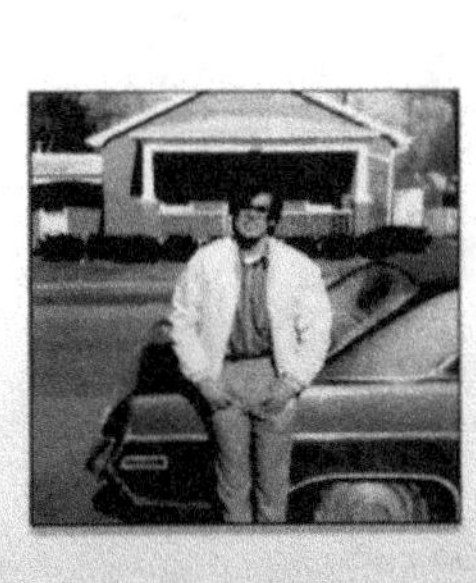
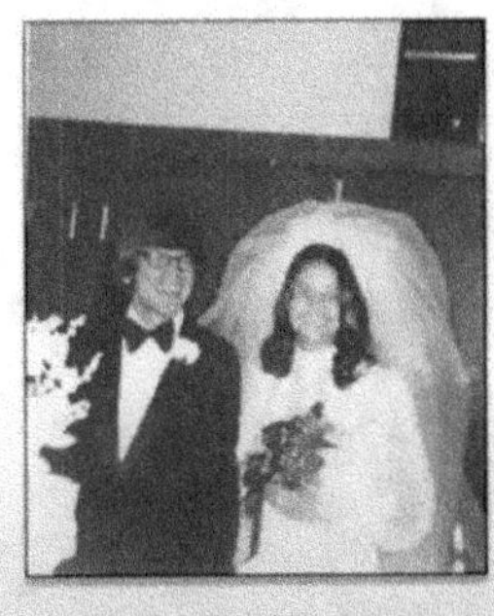
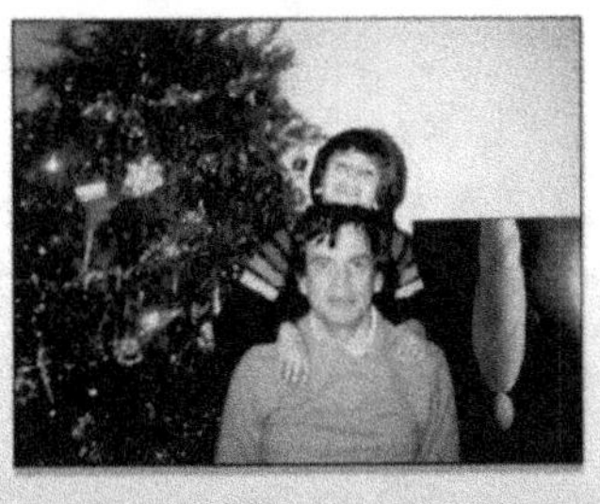

I realize at that moment that when we lost Dad, we not only lost him, but also *his stories, his empanada recipes and some pretty bad dad jokes.*

Unfortunately, *almost fifty million people here in the US lose someone close to them each year,* and they likely struggle to preserve those memories too. Perhaps they have an *old shoe box full of photos or a voicemail they leave on a phone*, but it's just not enough!

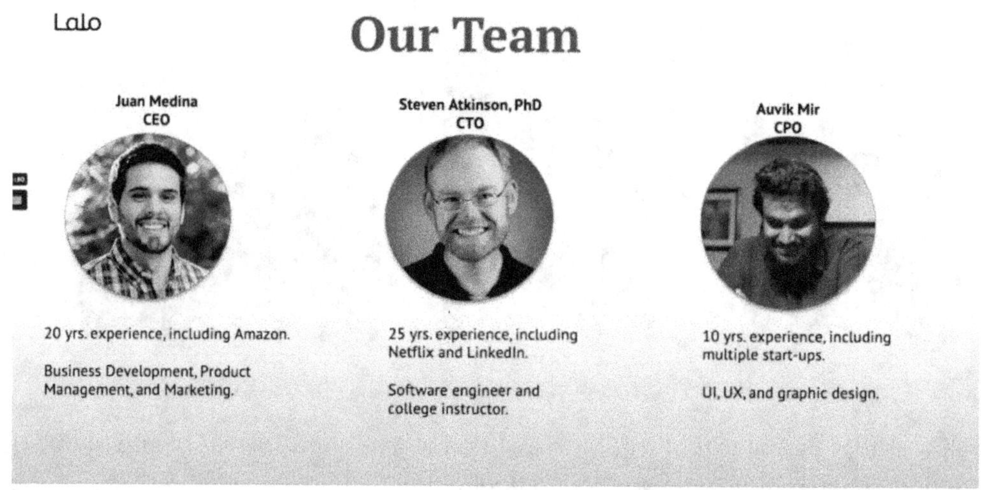

So, I'm introducing to you today: Lalo, named after *my father*, a place to *preserve family stories*. You can share memories using *videos, images or text*. We provide *video chat that you can record and play back at any time*, and conversation prompts to help you discover new stories all for $25 a year.

We have an experienced team with over fifty years of engineering, design, and business development experience both at start-ups and big companies like *Amazon and LinkedIn*.

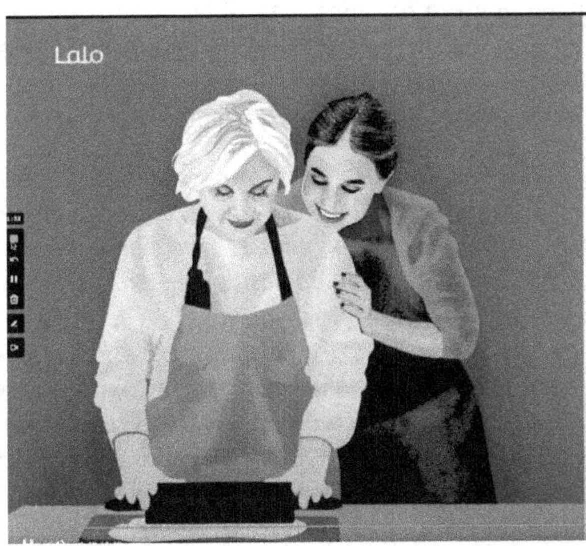

We have traction. The Portland Institute of Loss has agreed to distribute our app to their *fifteen hundred therapists*. We have over *two-thousand followers* between *Facebook and Twitter* and over *200 sign-ups* on Lalo's app—all leading us in the *right direction* for our Beta launch scheduled for late August.

Today, we're asking for your investor support to use for Engineering and Marketing resources, and we can always use new Beta testers and you can sign up today on Lalo.app.

Thank you!

—Juan Medina, CEO/Founder, Lalo

Juan is not only a great visionary and leader, but he has some marketing moxie to boot. He then took his video and put it on his social media platforms, mostly Twitter where he has 1500+ followers. Juan said that *within hours*, he was seeing "likes" and "retweets" occur and then investors started contacting him. "We love what you're doing... How can I get in?" Juan felt like he was in a dream.

Ten days after he launched that ninety-nine-second, story-based pitch onto his social media, he closed over $210K in investor funds.

This is a *wonderful* story about the power of storytelling within an investment presentation. Juan went from $0 results and a lot of closed doors to over $200K in just ten days because his story *illuminated* his vision. He pulled his investors in both *emotionally, logically,* and *financially*! The calls he got were now warmer, but he still had lots of technical slides and cap tables to back up their mission, and those doors and conversations were opened just by him telling *his* story.

As the Founder, think of your investor journey like a sales funnel journey. The initial outreach is higher up and provides just enough information to get the listener to understand your concept, the market opportunity, and the team that will execute this vision, and you get them to care that this problem needs to be solved.

As interest develops, you will be pulling in more of those data slides to prove your case. So, you will need them all, but not all in one shot. I have seen so many presentations that dump everything on the audience in the first meeting. As mentioned earlier, think of it like dating. Would you start a first date sharing everything you want from life?

"Hi, nice to meet you. I'm in my fifties. Divorced. Two great kids. Love cats. Sports are okay, I'm really in it for the social. I want to find someone that loves me unconditionally and wants to travel the world with me as my work takes me places. So, you need to be in a job that lets you go where you want, when you want. I plan to buy a huge house and expect you to pay your portion because if we're going to be partners, well, then you need to pony up to your side. I eat mostly plant-based and it's okay if you don't, but it would be nice if I can move you over to my diet because that just makes shopping easier. And I come with cats and if you're allergic, well, you best get meds for that; I hear Benadryl works wonders. I don't want you to have small kids because I'm ready to be an empty nester. Oh, and when we get married, I want a pre-nuptial agreement; marriage really is a financial agreement, not so much a love agreement, and, well, I worked hard for my success, so you best not feel entitled to it too. When I die, please cremate me, but just know my family lives long, so retirement savings is key. I'd like to hear all about you now. Please pass the breadbasket."

Um…You better not.

Same controlled approach with your investor, client, and partner conversations: Be strategic. Get into their shoes. You have to set the problem and your solution up so that they remember and like you. Court each other. It's definitely a partnership. And as their interest in you and your idea grows, the questions grow. Questions show interest. Celebrate questions,

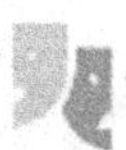

but don't try to anticipate all of them at once and make your slide deck work overtime. That's why having an Appendix is helpful. These are additional slides that may be helpful during anticipated Q&A that you can flip to after your formal presentation is done. Put some of the weeds you whacked upfront, into the Appendix, and make it nurturing compost.

CHAPTER SIXTEEN

KEYNOTES ARE STORYTELLING WITH PURPOSE

Congratulations, you've been invited to give a keynote to a huge room of people interested in your topic of expertise. You've been invited to speak for fifteen to forty-five minutes with you, a mic, and maybe a *red dot rug* under your feet. Those are keynotes. *Ted Talks, NAMI, Ignite Talks* are samples of amazing stories being shared with the world, so that when the keynote speaker has finished, they have provoked a new way of looking at something, and for many in the audience, cause an expansion in their awareness. A well delivered, authentic, and passionate keynote can change the world. Are you ready to start crafting yours?

I've had the honor of delivering two Ignite Seattle talks. Their slogan: *Enlighten us but make it fast.* And they ain't kiddin'. The speakers have exactly five minutes and must rotate automatically twenty slides that change every fifteen seconds. Talk about time constraint at its finest. This format is fun. It's challenging. And it's a delight to deliver one. What I love about these talks is that the speaker can teach through storytelling. The speaker would not have thought of this topic *without having experienced it personally in some way*, and we must know *that* story! They can be serious, silly, inspirational, motivational, curious, and mysterious. And they all educate and entertain. And they all come from passion.

In my own keynotes, I've talked about the challenges of OCD; Transgender Support in the LGBQT community (because I'm the proud parent of a trans child); as well as produced a storytelling show to advocate for anti-racism with a show we called "Melanin Stories Matter" and we spotlighted Black, Indigenous, and People of Color to tell their stories of racist moments and how they got through them (because after George Floyd, Brianna Taylor, and Ahmad Amory, I couldn't just stand there quiet and complicit!)

You may already know what your topic will address and now we just need to find the stories that go along with it as we gently blend in the data to support your idea, and deliver it so professionally, dramatically, and effectively, that you change lives! These keynotes can be used in Town Halls, annual company gatherings, or industry conferences. Keynote speakers are in high demand, and they can pay very well, so if this interests a dream you have, then this chapter may need a highlighter if you're reading the book version; the journal to sketch your outline; and the audible to hear samples of a keynote story being delivered.

WHAT KEYNOTE IS INSIDE OF YOU?

Does the idea that you have a topic that can change the world sound exciting? Well, now you have the tools to construct a beautiful and flowing talk that leads the listeners to pay attention to your wisdom and act. Let us make it captivating and effective for everyone hearing it. And it starts with you, Storyteller!

So, let's break it down to make it easy and joyous to create:

1. FIND A WORKING TITLE THAT CAPTURES THE ESSENCE OF WHAT YOU ARE GOING TO TEACH

As you've daydreamed about your keynote, your main mission is to teach us something that you know a lot about. Keynotes can address anything, and there will be an audience for it. You want your title to give the audience the outcome that you'll deliver them, so they are mentally prepped for the experience and welcoming the content. If your title is vague or overly clever, complicated, or off the topic you're addressing, you might frustrate some of your audience, and that is not a good move for your personal brand. So be clear about the outcome of what they will learn.

Exercise: Jot down a few titles just to get your focus on the content brewing. Here are some samples:

- Think and Grow Rich!
- Untap Your Unlimited Potential
- Five Ways to Get Out of Debt—and Stay Out
- Learn Storytelling for Business Professionals
- Master Emotionally Connected Leadership Through Your Storytelling
- Create the Life You Want Deliberately

2. DRAFT AN OUTLINE OF THE OVERALL TALK

Just like your individual stories have C.R.O.W. and senses deliberately plotted out, your *entire talk* needs that same approach. Look at the talk like an orchestration to the emotional result you seek in their limbic brains. Think of the draft as solidifying your *why and purpose* of giving this talk. Your draft will evolve as you dig into the stories and details, but the first draft is important because it will flow out more freely if you trust it and not overthink it.

Perhaps you want to start off with a story that is poignant and personal. That opening story is vital—as it is our intro to you as the speaker—and *why* you know what you know about this topic. The opening story is our first impression and must hook the audience right away. So, choose it and craft it carefully using the process in this book.

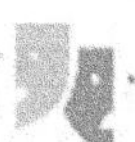

CONCLUDE YOUR STORIES WITH KEY TAKEAWAYS

When you conclude this first story (and all subsequent stories), you move into the *"What I learned from that moment?"* This is where you summarize the gold of your wisdom, and your slides move from emotional images to bullet points or even a statistic. And guess what is happening with your audience's minds? That's right, you're connecting with them both emotionally and logically because now your talk is balanced. Your neocortex and limbic brains are in concert, and now as the Storyteller, you have all the power and obligation to honor your audience's interest in your topic.

The next story builds upon the first story; and the third story builds upon the second—as you drive your points home to your conclusion and your Call to Action.

3. CHOOSE YOUR STORIES THAT SUPPORT YOUR POINT OF VIEW

Write, record, and storyboard *each story* so that it follows the story arc you've been taught in this book. This process will take time because each story needs to have C.R.O.W. and sensorial elements to mesmerize their Mind Movies. *Enjoy the journey* of crafting these stories that will thread your talk together. I suggest you return to some of the prompts found throughout this book and the accompanying journal to see if new stories are bubbling up now that you've decided to do a keynote!

4. SUMMARIZE THE BUSINESS POINT AFTER EACH STORY WITH A SEPARATE SLIDE

All stories must have a point and hopefully your *why*-you-do-what-you-do! All of this emotionally connected leadership drives the speaker to promote their personal authority brand, their organization, and their *why*.

YOUR CALL-TO-ACTION IS IMPORTANT

When you conclude your talk, what do you want them to do? That's the time to inspire such action. Ask them to participate in making real change in your company, or globally get involved if your mission spans the planet. QR codes that take them to sign up, or book time, or join a community that builds change is perfectly placed in your Call-To-Action. QR code participation helps you sherpa those that want to follow your ideas further. Lead them to the next part of your journey and mission.

5. CREATE A MASTER TALK STORYBOARD

Storyboards are fluid and never set in stone, but they are so helpful when you use them to craft bigger talks. Now that you have an outline of your talk, and a good idea of the matching story to prove your points, then create a Master Talk Storyboard. This will help you literally see the flow of your talk from one story, to the next. Here's a sample:

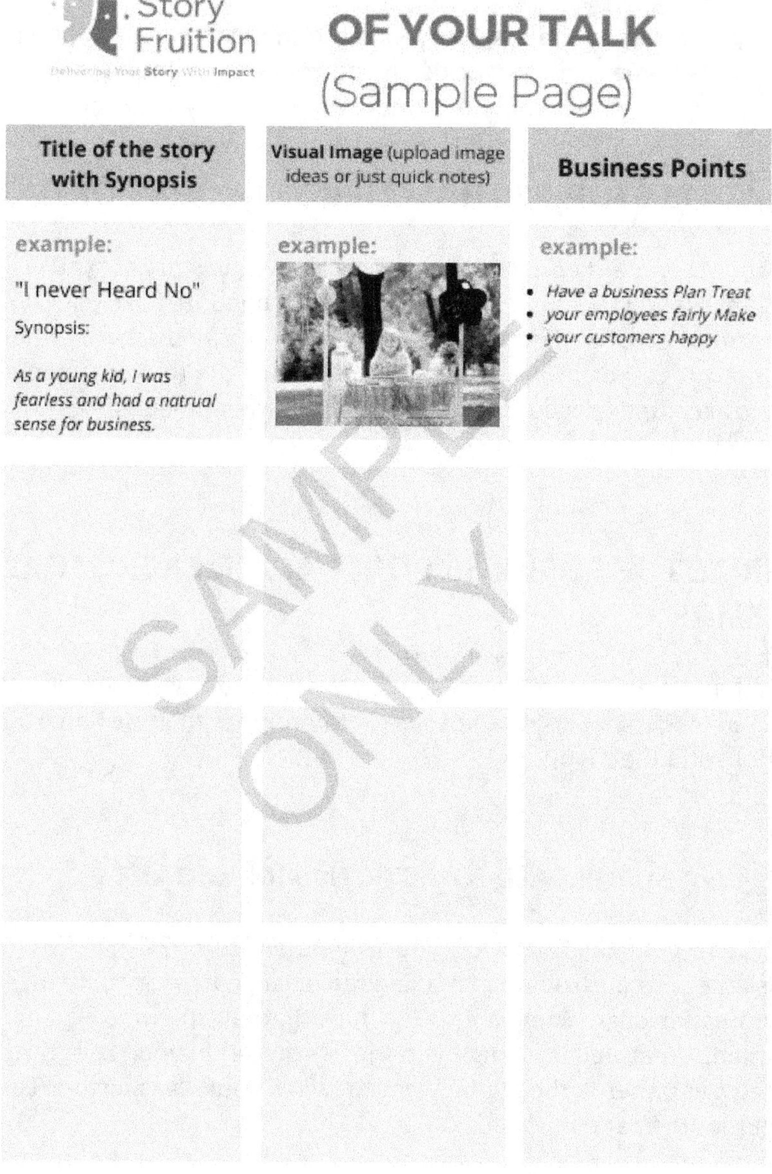

6. FIND YOUR TRANSITIONS

This step may come at the very end, but at least be thinking about your transitions between stories because we want it to shift smoothly and not like a stick shift on a hilly road.

Transition sentences leap off the last recap moment as you lead your audience to the next story. An example: *"As I realized that I needed to quit my high-paying job, never look back, and embrace entrepreneurship head on, I wasn't aware of the gifts I'd notice because I could see it from a third party set of eyes… let me introduce you to Brian a quiet genius just sitting in his zoom room box."*

Then change slides to represent the next story and start the process again:

- Story and image that supports the essence of the story
- Bullet point summary slide
- Transition sentence to lead to the next story, that further elevates your core message

7. PICK YOUR VISUALS CAREFULLY

As I have shared throughout this book, the slides are really important, and if you have visuals for your talk, pick them carefully. This is where they either support you or usurp you—and the choo-choo train of attention derails. Either outcome is of *your* doing.

One of my private clients who I met through LeadHERship Global, Lisa L Levy, the CEO of L-Cubed Consulting, hired Story Fruition to help her polish her storytelling skills and help craft a forty-five minute keynote around her expertise centering on organizational disruptions and how to tap the power of people, processes, and technology to respond quickly and efficiently.

Lisa has many stories from her robust career, and as we built her Story Library up, we then arranged them in a flowing order to create her signature talk to extend her consulting offerings with her keynote.

The goal is to have a talk that is educational, entertaining, and flows with relevant and helpful business tips.

- All slides have simple visuals for Story and Summary Slides
- Carefully crafted transition line that then connects her to the next story
- Rinse and repeat—until you get to your final story, then your Call to Action (CTA)
- CTA: Make sure they can get in touch with you! Invite them to the QR Code and lead them to your CRM system.
- Nurture the lead and close more business

The following is illustrating a part of her talk where we go from story one to story two:

Story Slide One: ROLLER COASTER: *The story of Lisa's realization that she no longer could or wanted to get on the corporate or start-up roller coaster anymore. She wanted to thrive in life, but this current point in her career had far too many twists, turns, and crazy descents. (three minutes)*

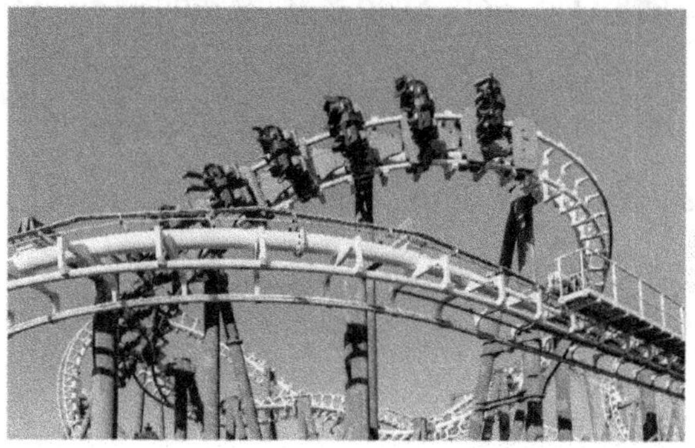

ROLLER COASTER SUMMARY SLIDE

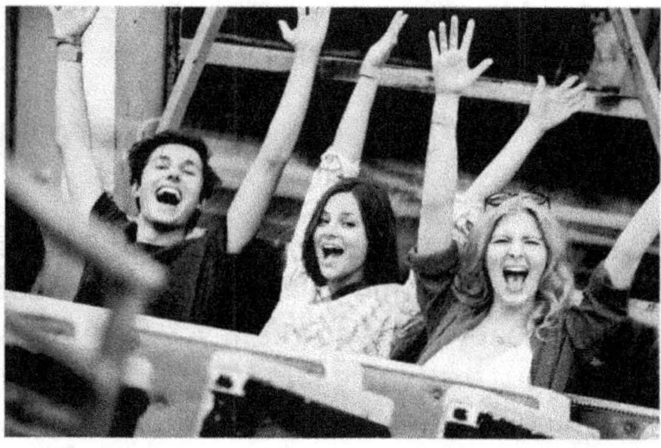

LISA'S TRANSITION LINE BEFORE NEXT STORY:

"Be patient with the ride. You cannot force the outcomes. Sometimes we have to downshift to remain in control."

Story Slide Two: KICKIN' IT OLD SCHOOL: *Lisa sits between two hospital operations teams and they all must learn to use new technology that runs like a stick shift, and not a Porsche on automatic (which is what they were used to using). So, frustration and tensions are high. How does Lisa navigate them with this new stick-shift model? (four minutes)*

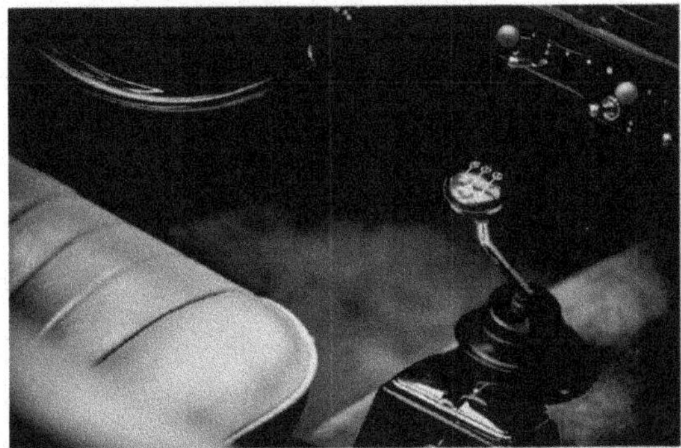

KEYNOTES WITHOUT VISUALS

Sometimes we only have our words and body language to create the Mind Movie we desire in our keynotes. Linda Fisk is an impressive leader. She's the Founder and CEO of LeadHERship Global, a networking group that connects women, those who identify as women, and male allies to participate more intimately with other CEOs and entrepreneurs.

Being a groundbreaker is in Linda's DNA. She holds a PhD in Clinical Psychology; multiple awards for her leadership; is a bestselling author and keynote speaker, and she's just a genuinely fantastic person to know. It was no surprise that TEDx would find her and ask her to speak, so she chose to follow her passion about enabling women and young girls to believe in themselves and rise up from some of the current ashes that this world brings to many girls in dire straits. Linda's mission is to change that and balance out the human energies, so that our economy thrives as a result of young women's minds being given the same opportunities as anyone else. To do this, Linda's talk on "Ladder Economics," opened with a story that hits hard to establish her first point, and her words, along with her pristine delivery, created powerful images. Here's an excerpt:

LADDER ECONOMICS, BY LINDA FISK, TEDX SWANSEA

Let me tell you a story that's all too common.

SET UP: LIFE AS MARIA KNOWS IT

Maria was fourteen, living in a small, isolated town in Colombia surrounded by gigantic mountains and deep ravines, and began working as a nanny for a well-to-do family at a neighboring town.

Maria walked three miles, in the sweltering heat, through a vast tropical jungle and across a slow-moving river to get to work by 6:00 a.m. every day. Although Maria dreamed of going to school, her village was considered one of the poorest and most remote in the country and had the sad privilege of hosting a large population of homeless people, begging on the street.

INCITING EVENT

After about a year, the family that employed Maria invited her to travel with them to the United States to care for their four children, and they promised to help Maria pursue her dream of getting an education. So, Maria, and her family, happily agreed. Maria got a two-year domestic-worker visa, and a few weeks later, she boarded a plane to Boston carrying one, small carry-on suitcase, and a Spanish–English dictionary. She didn't know it then, but Maria would become a survivor of labor and sex trafficking.

RISING ACTION (CONFLICT)

Maria was told that she owed $12,000 for the visa, and her transportation to the United States. Only then did Maria find out that she would get paid just $25 per week. So, Maria would have to work for the family for ten years to pay off her debt. Her passport was taken away from her and she worked eighteen hours a day, seven days a week with no days off.

Sometimes the parents had guests visit, and Maria had to cook and clean for them too. None of the guests ever said a word to her. She was a fixture in the house; a robot; there to do things for them. Maria felt invisible, dispensable, and alone. And soon, her traffickers started expecting Maria to be available, sexually, to their guests, as well. This went on for two years.

And, while we might like to think that slavery is a thing of the past, in the twenty-first century, the opposite is true.

DATA INFUSION

There are over 28.7 million women and girls across the world caught up in the modern-day slave trade. Today. Right now. And a third of the world's poorest girls, aged between ten and eighteen, have never been to school.

Today. Right now.

There are 130 million girls who are completely missing out on school. And about 650 million girls and women - alive today - were married as a child, under the age of fifteen.

VISION

Our world of tomorrow depends on whether the leaders of today, and all who stand with them, recognize the urgency and peril of inaction. Leaders and decision-makers, whether in South Sudan or the South Side of Chicago, need to demand physical and psychological safety and equal access to basic human rights: nutrition, ability to control their bodies, to choose a mate, and access to health care, education, jobs, and housing - for all girls and all women, everywhere.

CALL TO ACTION

It is up to all of us, who stand upon the shoulders of so many, to push and hold wide open the doors of opportunity. Ensuring every girl and every woman has the possibility of leading life to her fullest potential.

We are at a critical juncture in human history, which could lead to widely contrasting futures. But I am convinced that the future is not set in stone. It's flexible, bendable, and adaptable, and dependent on our actions.

Right here. Right now.

In one future, by recognizing and protecting the physical and psychological safety of girls and women around the world, and giving them access to basic human rights, half of the world's population – millions of people - could be lifted out of poverty!

This new wealth could empower millions of families, adding significantly to local and national economies. The global economy could nearly double by 2030 - to $132 trillion in

today's currency. Innovations could dramatically improve physical and mental health, new discoveries and inventions could continue to improve and impact human lives. We ALL benefit.

—Linda Fisk, CEO LeadHERship Global, Author, Keynote Speaker, TEDx Swansea, June 2022

Wow! That's opening with a bang and sets the stage for Linda's passion as she launches the point of her talk. This TEDx talk was especially exciting in that Linda filmed it in Dallas while TV producers sent Linda's image as a *hologram* to Sweden. So, yes, add that to your public speaking bucket list and become a hologram!

Keynotes are meccas for storytelling, and this is some of my favorite work to do with clients because it's a platform where they get to tell *their* story and tell it well! Let's find yours.

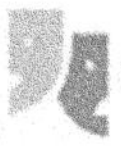

RECAP OF PROCESS FOUR:

- Investor, sales, and boardroom decks tell the story with you. Make sure the slides support you and do not usurp you by being too busy. We don't need to know your entire journey as an entrepreneur. Just enough to decide if we believe in your mission and support it in money, time, or equity.
- Each presentation page tells a story and is not just a stats/data dump on the listeners.
- When crafting a longer keynote, you can make a "Master Storyboard" for your talk that then has individual storyboards for the chosen stories.
- Keep your images simple and offer recap or key takeaways after each story concludes.
- Have smooth story transitions to let the audience know you are changing gears.

PERFORMANCE AND DELIVERY

LOCKING IN YOUR MIND MOVIE

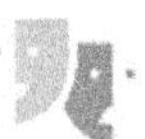

CHAPTER SEVENTEEN

REHEARSE, REHEARSE, REHEARSE!

I'm walking out of the theater, having just delivered an awesome show to a full house in San Diego, when someone in the audience genuinely asked, "How do you remember all those lines?" I giggled and said, "We rehearse."

So, you've now learned story-mining, story-crafting, story-boarding, and weed whacking are the parts of a journey of a Storyteller, but all of that goes out the window if you don't rehearse. **Rehearsal drills the details into your mind,** and the delivery is what ignites the Mind Movie into your listeners' heads. I love to rehearse and do it while on walks as I record multiple times, adjusting for dialogue needs, character development, and takeaway points. Rehearsal is the most playful state of the process and one that I hope you embrace and appreciate more in time.

When working with a private client, I start off as a journalist mining their life; then morph to a storyboard artist to craft their story; and then finally into a director, helping them bring out their best performance every time. This is where the power of voice tone, pacing, and body language all come into play. It's the final art you sprinkle into your presentation as the Storyteller. Your "Faceless clients in the case study," move to "Rich characters in your *Case Stories.*" Dialogue brings them to life and the audience will delight in your entertaining and educational presentation. No one wants to be lectured to so embracing the theatrics will create a captivating delivery that people can retain far longer than drab delivery with little human connections or emotion.

If you choose to "wing it" and hope it works out, you are risking a lot. I'm highly trained in improv, so my ability to "wing it" is a muscle that I've spent decades working, but I still always rehearse. So, if you don't have that improv skill in your toolbox, then rehearsal will:

- Reduce your nerves.
- Increase your confidence
- Allow for more vivid images to occur in your listeners' minds
- Shows respect to your audience
- Strengthens your own personal brand because your audience sees you are clearly prepared.

REHEARSAL FEEDBACK BUDDIES

Rehearsal needs to happen on your own time, but it's also good to mix in either a storytelling coach or someone you can trust who will give you honest and direct feedback. If you are turning to a trusted friend or colleague, ask them to watch for some of the following.

As the speaker, am I:

1. Sharing my stories so that they are easy to follow? (Story arc of transformation.)
2. Do I get confusing anywhere and derail the train (causing Wonder/Wander)?
3. When I'm doing dialogue, can you differentiate from the characters talking? If not, then make sure you fine tune the voices more.
4. Are my slides clean and supportive? Or are they crowded and confusing?
5. Is my ending concise with clear Calls to Action for this talk? (What do you want them to do after they hear your words?)
6. How's my time? Am I in the requested time allocation? *If not, then you must edit your words, which can be editing out scenes. Choose a more concise language to paint the pictures. Sometimes it could be a pacing issue too.*
7. Am I mixing it at different tempos? Slowing down for serious or key points; speeding up for time travel montages. Pausing to give the audience a catch-up break? Or, is it all one pace and tone? (That can get monotonous.)

TAKE THEIR FEEDBACK TO HEART.

Detach and know that they are making you even better because they'll see things you may be missing. As you continue to craft and sculpt this story, your third-party helper(s) will be platinum gold for your work!

THE POWER OF THE PAUSE

Let's pause...to talk about the *power* of...the pause. That beautiful silent moment when the presenter stops and says nothing for a few moments is mesmerizing. What happens with the audience's experience as a result of that pause? So much. The audience can catch up, take a breath, revel in the Mind Movie images you've created, allow for tears, feel empathy, feel excitement, and lean into you. *"What is she going to say next?"*

> *In that dramatic pause, you have the listener's full attention as they wait for your next move.*
> *Milk it and entertain them.*

Creating deliberate places to pause for impact is strategic, like a game of chess. When you deliver a line that you *know* will jar their thinking in some way, it's like you moved the Queen into a checkmate space. Remember, your listeners are also writing their own story as they follow your story. They are listening intently. **The Power of The Pause** is a beautiful gift for your listeners—so much happens in that silence. Just choose it *carefully* and avoid over-using it. Too many pauses can make you appear boring or artificial, which can make people check out.

Here's one of my personal journey's done in ninety-nine seconds; it travels twenty-four years, and I use pausing to switch gears. If you have the Audio book, you'll hear the pauses more easily.

TWO HANDS

I'm on my honeymoon in Hawaii. We're so excited to be married because now we will walk through life together, hand-in-hand!

We're sitting at a luau, enjoying delicious pork pulled from the sandy ground and wrapped in banana leaves with purple potatoes and fresh salads. Our new table mates are a bit corny when they over-enthusiastically introduce themselves. "Hi, I'm Sandy!" she says. "And I'm Jack!" he says. "And we're the Jones'! We're celebrating our thirtieth wedding anniversary!"

We can't help but notice that Jack doesn't have a hand. It's a stump from an accident some time ago, and he's cool with it. It makes for interesting table banter, but we move on from the topic to something else. It was a lovely night. **(Small pause).**

The next day… I must have more of that pig.

We return to the same luau with a completely different crowd and new table mates. My husband turns his head to me and says, very discreetly, like a ventriloquist, "The man doesn't have a hand."

"WHAT?!" I yelp, not expecting that piece of information, and I look to see that –indeed—he did *not* have a hand! *What is going on here? Two different handless men in a row?*

"Okay, so this is weird. Spiritual things happen in threes and that's two," so I start looking around to see if someone else doesn't have a hand. *And what does this all mean?* It's too weird not to pay attention to. But for years we couldn't figure out the symbolism.

(Small pause and change in voice tone to more serious.)

Twenty years later, our marriage had receded like the waves hitting the shores of Hawaii.

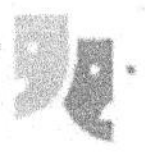

> **(Longer pause because I'm about to time travel and change scenery.)**
>
> I'm sitting in a park in Bellevue with my husband. He asks, "So, are we done?"
>
> "Yes, we're done."
>
> As we're standing up, a woman walks out of the public bathroom. She… doesn't have a hand.
>
> **(Pause.)**
>
> We stand up.
>
> And single-handedly…
>
> walk towards…divorce.

This a story of joy at the beginning, and then in just ninety-nine seconds swoops to the loss of the marriage with all the wisdom of twenty-four years wrapped up in that single moment when the woman walks out of the bathroom. The story lands on sadness, but when included in my one-woman show, the next story would begin my triumph and resilience.

Side note: Divorce stories are rich. It can be the divorce of a marriage or of a business partnership because they are stories of one chapter ending and a new one on unchartered waters beginning. These are stories of change, fighting it, and then accepting it, and producing new versions of oneself.

TIME CONSTRAINTS NEED TO BE HONORED—SO REHEARSE, PLEASE.

When you are asked to deliver a talk, you'll likely be told how much time they want it to take. Please honor it. And the more you rehearse and time yourself, the cleaner your talk becomes.

BOOK REHEARSAL TIME ON YOUR CALENDAR AND HOLD YOURSELF ACCOUNTABLE TO DOING IT.

Time allocation will let you know how many stories you can include or not include. The longer time you have been given, the more stories and details you can include as you weave your business points throughout the talk.

A forty-five-minute talk, for example, can be broken into three fifteen-minute sections. That might be three well-crafted stories with a business summary at the end of each. Or

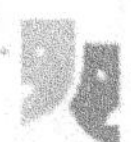

it could be six stories and business points that all land around seven minutes each. If you are only given five minutes to speak, that tends to be *one* story only, but you can tell it very vividly.

If you are given only three minutes, it needs to be one story, but with more weed whacking to get the words and dialogue very precise.

Shorter time can feel harder because of the precision. My Founders Live clients see that all the time when we tell them they only have ninety-nine seconds to share how they are going to change the world, but we get it done. In ninety-nine seconds we deliver:

1. **Problem Narrative:** The opening story with a character experiencing "the problem."
2. **Solution:** Intro to your company's remedy.
3. **The Addressable Market:** Data dropped in during the narrative, and sometimes graphs.
4. **Go to Market Strategy:** How you'll find these customers.
5. **Pricing/Business Model:** How you'll make money.
6. **The Team: IMPORTANT!** Proof you're the team to do this. Have you started and sold a company before? Tell that story too
7. **The Ask:** What you seek from them, be it funding, advising, promotion.

We tend to break the first thirty seconds to do the problem; and that leaves one minute, nine seconds to do two-seven. It's doable and well worth having a *quick pitch* in your Story Library. You'll use it a lot and know it's a higher-level story of what you do. The subsequent presentations fill in more details with more data or the science of your business. This is where you, as the Founder and CEO, strut your industry knowledge stuff while the questions are being fired at you. The key is to balance the data with the narrative. **C.R.O.W. has a place in all of these time allotments.**

HUMOR IS SOMETIMES *SERIOUSLY* NEEDED

All great stories show us transformation, and that is never a straight linear line. We have highs and lows, twists and turns, and even the most serious story must make room for a little humor. If you don't provide some moments of relief after a heavy or exciting story, then your audience may go "into the fetal position" as I like to say. They could feel sad and overwhelmed and maybe even sad for you. You have the Storyteller's *obligation* to educate and entertain and humor makes that journey softer.

Where you place the humor can be like a game of chess once again. You could be funny just before you hit them with a shocking moment, which elevates surprise. Or you can find it after the big moment, to show your human side, and provide relief for the listener so they see you're all right. In the movie, *Raiders of the Lost Arc*, Indiana Jones just went through hell and back in one of his adventurous scenes, when he stops, thinking all was okay, and snakes appear to torment him further. The timing of the line is hilarious and much appreciated after the audiences' hearts have been racing from all the action. Indiana Jones (played by Harrison Ford) says deadpan:

"Snakes. Why did it have to be snakes?"

Find your humor-needed moments as they will only enhance the adventure you have your keynote listening audience on.

PERFORMANCE TAKES COMMITMENT

The key reason to rehearse is to confidently impress and inspire your audiences. This part takes dedication, and the more you practice, the stronger your talk becomes and the more you know it, which builds confidence, which allows you to be more relaxed and playful when delivering it. I've said it before, but it stands saying again:

> *Rehearsal is a presenter's best friend*

There are a few ways to learn from your rehearsal. To really get the most out of each session is to **audio record** and play it back. Why audio only at times? Because when you are on a podcast or radio interview, you *only* have your voice. You want to know what you sound like prior, don't you? So, let's make sure it sounds warm and inviting. I record while I'm on a walk using my phone—or just in a quiet space undisturbed for a set amount of time. Then I play it back, take mental notes to try new things, and then re-record to improve upon the last draft.

If you want to practice slides, then you'll need **video and screen-sharing technology** to practice how you maneuver the mouse, animations, videos, etc. If this is a *virtual presentation*, then you'll also want to decide if your face is large screen and split with your slides, vs your image in a tiny box in the corner of a zoom room while your slides take center stage. Practice how you want to finesse that. *Quick tips to watch for in your audio and video recordings:*

- **Pacing:** Find places to go fast or slow and when to return to a more even pace makes your talk have variety, which keeps it interesting.
- **Voice tonalities:** When you are in dialogue with characters, make sure that we can tell the difference.
- **Body language:** If this is live presentation on stage, you have the luxury of being able to use your arms, legs, and full body to help further the emotional connection. If this is a virtual presentation, you may want to stand up; or if sitting, then lean in and work the camera more deliberately. For a dramatic or comedic moment, try leaning into the camera as if you are "getting in their face or space," and you'll provide entertainment.
- **Staging:** I look at this part of delivery like a play or a choreographed dance. Where do you plan to physically stand for your talk? Look at where the monitors are and the sound system and find a spot where you'll not block either. Know when you would

be blocking and avoid doing it by creating a mental chalk line that you can't cross. I *recommend minimal stage movement*, like random pacing, because it only distracts from your power. Stand still and take control of the room. When you do move, it has purpose, like indicating to the audience by a step or two, that you're stepping into your next story.

- **Lighting:** A smart investment is to get a light for your zoom meetings; or just have good lighting in *front* of your face. We want to see you and not in the shadows, which always looks creepy. If you're doing a stage talk, look for where the stage shadows begin, and use that mental chalk of yours again to keep you in the light.
- **Microphone:** It will mean nothing if we cannot hear or understand you, so using a mic properly is essential.
  - o **Handheld microphone:** I advise to hold it by your *chin* so that your voice reaches it easily. Remember to have the mic follow your chin anytime you move. *Do not turn your head without your mic going with you.* I see this far too much. The most common is when the speaker keeps turning around to look at their slides when their monitor in front of them is all you need.
  - o **Headset mic:** Great! Just make sure not to bump the mic if it's clipped on a jacket. The mic positioned by your mouth is most ideal in my experience.
  - o No matter what the mic is, you need to be very cognizant that you are speaking clearly and at a volume we can tolerate. Too low or too loud are equally distracting and will derail the train.

As you mix variety into your presentations, you'll be activating more of those neurotransmitters we talked about earlier in "Your Brain On Story." Just please, be gentle with yourself as you rehearse. Your early drafts won't be polished yet. They'll even be rocky at first. Your time will likely be too much, or not enough; you'll not know if the order is working like you thought it would, so just shuffle them around. You'll also struggle with the transition lines, but they will come! Creating a keynote is exciting, an honor, and takes commitment, but worth it when you're going to change the world with it. Rehearse and then step confidently up on that world stage and *own it*!

RECAP PROCESS FIVE: PERFORMANCE

1. Rehearsal is your best friend and will help you build confidence as you refine your presentation. Each iteration will get better!
2. Use a variety of ways to record and get feedback: Audio, video and Feedback Buddies who will give you objective input (vs your mom's).
3. Honor time constraints, and when you rehearse, you will make your time allotment more frequently.
4. Be aware of your microphone and lighting when in performance. Draw an imaginary chalk line to keep you being seen and heard nicely.
5. If you don't rehearse enough, you will be adding unnecessary stress and affect your delivery negatively. Get in front of it and be ready to deliver your talk at least three days before it's due.

BUILDING YOUR STORY LIBRARY

HOW TO ORGANIZE YOUR STORIES FOR EASY ACCESS BOTH FOR YOURSELF, AND YOUR TEAMS

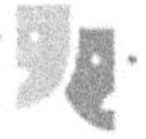

CHAPTER EIGHTEEN

STORY LIBRARIES

Congratulations on all the stories you now have percolating for public consumption. But now what? You are going to need a library to file your stories for your own personal use for talks, interviews, and keynotes as well as creating a group repository for your organization to access and share for other purposes. Core stories to build and create in your Story Library are:

- **Company/Brand Story**
- **Founder's Origin Story (Your Story Fruition, and maybe a few versions of it)**
- **Client Case Stories (Nonprofits need to build these stories up too!)**
- **Vision Stories (Board meetings, Town Halls, sales meetings, Mergers and Acquisitions)**
- **Marketplace Stories (Stories of other companies' successes and failures)**
- **Leadership Stories**
- **Human Resource Success Stories**
- **C-Suite Leadership Stories**

One of my mentors and friend, Kane Minkus, a brilliant storyteller and CEO of Industry Rockstars, teaches entrepreneurs how to get their businesses to soar to the top as quickly as possible. He teaches how Marketplace Stories explain the state-of-affairs in the industry as well as stories of what other brands have done to address a problem and the outcomes. These Marketplace Stories are powerful because they show your Big Picture global awareness and are not completely centered just on you and your organization. Perhaps sharing a Steve Jobs success story, such as when he revolutionized our relationship with technology, may be worth putting into your library. Or how Richard Branson saw the pain point in the airline industry and knew that he could elevate customer experience with hip flight attendants, massage chairs for first class, and dancing musical videos for the safety speech. And that's how Virgin America was born. He broke a paradigm, and maybe your company is doing something similar. Infusing Marketplace stories has a place in your Story Library.

CONTINUOUSLY BUILD YOUR STORY LIBRARY

Your Story Library will become your greatest resource asset. People relate to leaders who are *real*, not afraid to share vulnerable moments, and who know how to use stories to highlight lessons learned and wisdom gained.

As an organization, having this Story Library repository is providing access to company knowledge. Your team can learn who the leaders are and what they value; how your company evolved; and who your best customers are all in this training space.

Sharing your stories across your organization, or just your own personal Story Library, is not hard to do. Story Libraries are highly valuable because they unite teams and expand their company knowledge. Everyone can easily access this knowledge through the digital Story Library where they'll find storyboards and videos of the story being told at optimum delivery. For example:

- Sales may need a Sales Engineer who has stories from a variety of clients that can be shared by both teams.
- A new salesperson can learn the company's brand story faster and numerous case stories to hit the ground running.
- Human Resources can share stories about leadership or successful HR programs for more people during onboarding.
- Founders can include their own Story Fruition to infuse at Investor Meetings.
- The C-Suite needs to know key vision stories for the next shareholders meeting.

How you classify the stories is up to each organization, but just make sure your navigation is user friendly and intuitive. For example, if you are setting up a section for Success Stories, then you may want to have sub-categories like: Finance Success Stories, Health Success Stories, etc. Or, perhaps you want your leaders to be given their own channel. Stories from the Founder/CEO, CFO, CMO, COO, etc. If you are interested in Story Fruition to help you build your Story Library, simply go to our website and book time.

NINETY-NINE-SECOND STORIES

In a keynote, or a Town Hall, you will have the luxury of telling longer stories, but in many presentations, you must be quick to make the point, so **let's raise the bar to ninety-nine seconds.** Why? Because our attention spans are short, and you don't necessarily need more time to deliver a great business story *with impact*. Any story that you build that is longer than ninety-nine seconds can still be trimmed down. Think about Netflix or YouTube that boils the entire show down into one sentence. It just takes precision and thoughtful word choices.

To create a ninety-nine-second story, let's follow the narrative arc that Story Fruition embraces: the Hero's Journey. It's an easy arc to follow and here is the graphic to remind you:

Your Story of Transformation

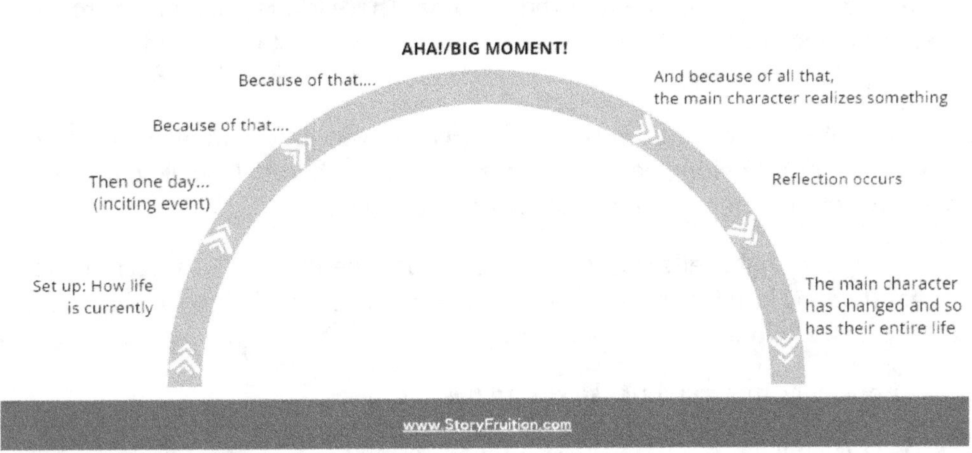

You'll need to have a beginning (C.R.O.W.), a middle (the adventure), and an ending with meaning and key points to give your audience. For an investor or partner pitch, the ending is usually your KPIs attained, happy customer testimonials, and your *ask.* That's a lot, but we can do it. You just need to choose your words wisely and paint every scene with vivid images that create emotional connection for the listeners. The more of these quick stories your company builds, the more content your teams have in their Story Library.

A NINETY-NINE-SECOND STORY IS APPROXIMATELY 250-300 WORDS.

If you are going to tell it slower, using pauses for dramatic effect, then it's better to lean towards the 250-word count to give your story space. The goal here is to find personal or professional moments when you learned something about yourself. You were one person before the event, then you had the "Aha!" moment, and you were changed forever and became the new version of yourself.

Here is an example from one of the University of Washington-Tacoma LATIN X award winners for education in her community, Maria Luisa. We call this short story, "Bathroom Warrior," and she shared it as part of her acceptance speech at the Celebrando Comunidad. This moment in her young life transformed her career path trajectory, so therefore a story to definitely craft and perfect.

BATHROOM WARRIOR

I'm twelve years old and I'm standing in the bathroom of my middle school, a dingy room in the basement of the building. There is a familiar girl there with me; her name is Delia. She is small in stature, like me, standing in front of the mirror, pulling her long, dark hair into combs on either side of her head.

Two tall white girls, both older than us, walk in and immediately pick on Delia. "You don't belong here. Go home! Get out of here!" One violently grabs her combs out of her hair and throws them to the floor.

My flight or fight reflexes kick in. I step in between them like a warrior. I feel bigger than my four feet nine inches. "You don't have the right to say that to her, to Delia! She belongs. I know her. Now GO!"

Surprisingly, they run out like scared hyenas.

Delia is crying, "Why are they so mean to me?" I hug her. *"No lo se, pero somos Latinas, y somos igual. I don't know, but I understand. You belong here. I'm Latina too."*

I am aware for the *first time* that I have to use my own *White-Passing Privilege*. But I am still a Bathroom warrior, an interpreter, someone who connects and leans into my community.

I've dedicated my life to community development, that's what I think public health and education is all about. The University of Washington-Tacoma has called upon my connections in this community many times, as have others. At times it can be frustrating, as these are my deep connections, relationships that I have built over years. I sometimes want to protect that like a bathroom warrior.

—Maria Luisa, University of Washington-Tacoma

When Maria Luisa tells the story, she steps right into the scene. Her voice changes when she yells at the bullies, as does her body language; then a moment later, she is tender and soft as she comforts Delia. It's a beautiful and powerful story of a moment that affected Maria's life course. The twelve-year-old girl that walked out of that bathroom was a different girl. You could even say she was a blossoming young woman, just from that moment. That story of transformation is told in 274 words!

The set up in her C.R.O.W. is clear from the very first word. We instantly know her age in life so we can make lots of tween-angst assumptions. We can see her as a girl. We know where she is physically because we can all imagine a middle-school bathroom. We see the small girl with long dark hair, Delia, innocently putting the combs in her hair. All is normal in their lives.

INCITING EVENT:

The Bullies enter and pick on Delia and terror ensues. We can see two tall white girls, and it doesn't matter if they are blond, redhead, brunette; that's up to the listener to create, and why storytelling is so persuasive. Everyone is creating their own Mind Movie!

And because of that.... Maria Luisa quickly moves into her response…

And because of that …the Bullies run off like scared hyenas and Maria Luisa embraces Delia when she has her *Aha! Moment.* She realizes her White-Passing Privilege as a Latina has power over those who are darker in melanin.

Life Changed/Reflection: This moment in Maria Luisa's young life had a tremendous impact on her and she would later become a leader in Education in the LatinX community of Tacoma, WA. She walked into that bathroom as one person, and walked out another, wiser person, who would have a purpose. She is still a Bathroom Warrior today.

Airway Science for Kids, or ASK, is a nonprofit organization near to my heart. They help underserved communities receive much needed STEM (Science, Technology, Engineering, and Mathematics) curriculums focused on careers in Aviation and Aerospace. This industry is dominated by over 86 percent White males and is greatly underrepresented from Black, Indigenous and People of Color (also referred to as BIPOC)[1] and why diversity, equity, and inclusion is paramount in importance. The American school systems lack the funding for the proper educational resources in these typically lower-income schools. ASK is on a mission to change that and works with aviation-minded companies to sponsor and groom the next generations of gender-diverse and BIPOC pilots, aviation engineers, designers, and aeronautic mechanics.

Nonprofits survive on grants and donations, so they need to be great storytellers. Julia Cannell leads the way to ensuring that her team has a library of stories that they all learned when storytelling was needed for their donation drives and partnership ascertainment. Story Fruition taught the **Storytelling Workshop and Master Minds**. The Master Minds are small "pods" where five participants practice what they learned from the Storytelling Workshop. Master Minds put the knowledge to use in order to begin refining their communication skills. Each participant contributes two stories to their shared Story Library. Here's an example of one of Julia's "Executive Director stories" that shows her own Story Fruition. All of her senior leadership must know and be able to tell her background since she sits at the top. Potential partners and donors tend to want to have that information. In this sample, it's for Julia to use in a keynote and is in first person. Her staff obviously will convert it to third person and edit down some scenes. Two storyboards are necessary. One for Julia; one for her staff.

---

[1] https://www.yahoo.com/video/86-of-air-force-pilots-are-white-men-heres-why-this-needs-to-change-155046366.html?guc-counter=1&guce_referrer=aHR0cHM6Ly93d3cuZ29vZ2xlLmNvbS8&guce_referrer_sig=AQAAAGYhEsZwd8yhXWtp627JJd-m0i6vIKa4_b2qe9Q4T05prtM-9g5ECmrGN78O3zAFLjEOU2KCIF8YpVbVE6q1UpJE9SnI7Tb2RQJItgDd4fX09SP2UOGdQIi-YElt9-i7bv1TRl-Zk4ZkV4DiwXsV-TXlIuiRqfP8UZ8X59SA-8I8-2

OPEN DOORS

It is January 18, 1990, and I'm twenty-five years old, standing in the foyer of my home in Tacoma, WA. Over the last ten months, I have gotten married, graduated from college, and when I open the front door, I will become a mom.

A year ago, I was caught up in the bliss of wedding planning and the general euphoria that comes from being twenty-four, in love, and living in a single-wide trailer in Ellensburg, Washington. I was listening to my fiancé read a want ad from the *Seattle Times* (It's a newspaper. Really. They used to deliver those things.) "Wanted, Foster Parents. Homes needed for short-term placement of children ages 0-18. Training provided and expenses are covered."

The first problem with this was that I didn't know what a "foster child" was, but once I knew, I felt like it was something we should do.

The phone rings a few hours later. Did I realize that my house was big enough to take a family group? AND, since I had a multiracial family, I could be a culturally relevant placement for Asian youth. Why, no, I didn't. And now, I open the door to meet the three children that will be with me for *just six weeks*.

The door is made of glass, so I've been seen. There is no going back now. I cautiously turn the handle, cautious because I am a very tall woman, and these are very tiny children. I'm nervous I'll scare them. A six-year-old with the face (and voice) of an angel looks up at me and says, "Hi. Is this where we are going to live now? Can I see my room?"

I have *no* idea what I'm doing as a parent. Which is pretty much the story of my life. I know I'll figure it out as I go. You know how some parents teach you to swim by throwing you in the water? Mine put me on an airplane at sixteen and told me to go fly. Suffice to say that they raised me to have every confidence I could do anything. It was sometimes scary, but effective. In case you wanted to know, I am less afraid of flying 20,000 feet above the earth than I am of those tiny children.

The experience of raising foster children gives me insight into the challenges faced by parents raising their children in what has become my new reality. We lived in the neighborhoods that our children grew up in and the schools had high percentages of youth living on low incomes, English Language learners, and students with learning disabilities. I quickly realized that I have to find a way to help my kids because their teachers are overwhelmed. The resources they need are not available at their schools, and the quality of education is one that would not be tolerated in suburban schools. We need to Open Doors for them to thrive.

It is on a trip to Seattle's The Museum of Flight with my kids that sparks the idea that I can use aviation to educate and inspire my kids. ASK Founder, Robert Strickland, used to say we use aviation to *trick* kids into learning. That is what I do—I find creative ways to teach different subjects. Having a Museum of Flight membership is our one financial splurge, and I use it to the fullest. Airplanes function not on miles per gallon, but on

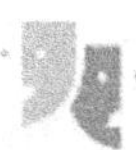

gallons of fuel used per hour. We make a game of choosing two locations (geography), discover how many gallons of fuel we will need to get there (math), find one unique fact about each airport (history), learn what weather we should prepare for (science and fashion), and how to plot the trip on a map.

You get the idea—you can discuss any subject without it sounding like school.

My master's education and experience in Aviation along with my unexpected role as a foster parent provided me with the unique set of skills that today I use to guide Airway Science for Kids—an organization focused on bringing Aerospace opportunities to all students. Raising children who were the definition of "historically underserved" while coming from my own background of growing up with so many advantages, opened my eyes to the gaping disparity in opportunities.

I am committed to the idea that everyone deserves to learn, dream, and have a career that they can be passionate about. At ASK, we bring the possibility to life and allow countless invisible children to be seen.

—Julia Cannell, Executive Director, Airway Science for Kids
Portland Oregon

As a former enterprise and start-up salesperson, I can tell you that having a repository of stories that someone can learn quickly is a smart investment. Stories not only help sell your products and services, but they also help foster trust with your employees faster and deeper because they can see your successes. They can learn your leadership's heart. Build your Story Library, and if you need help with it, contact us at Story Fruition.

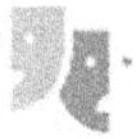

RECAP PROCESS SIX: STORY LIBRARIES

1. Filing your personal stories into your own digital Story Library preserves your stories via Storyboards, scripts and videos.
2. Companies can share stories using their own Story Library, so that storytelling becomes infused into their culture.
3. Fill your library with a variety of themes and time lengths. Some will be longer stories for keynotes, and some will be quick ones for more casual presentations.
4. Train your staff across the organization to utilize *and contribute* to your Story Library because that is both your history of successes, events, and vision for the future. Make them all accessible so that staff stays consistent with your messaging.
5. Master Mind pods allow your team to safely create and sculpt new stories for your Story Library, and how to perform them.

CHAPTER NINETEEN

NOT THE END... BUT TO BE CONTINUED...

Being a Founder, business professional, senior leader, visionary or a "Rising Star," it is exciting and takes bravery to step onto a stage, turn on a microphone, and bare it all. As you start to seed your idea and take it out to the world, you'll undoubtedly get a lot of feedback on how to run your business. Some of the advice will go against *your* Gut Instinct, and some of it will feel like it's exactly what you need.

Your desire to become a powerful Storyteller to enhance your emotionally connected leadership capabilities speaks volumes about your character. This book has hopefully helped you think differently about how to mesmerize your audiences. The more you hone your storytelling skills, the better you will become at everything you do, and you'll never go back to bland imagery or relying on emotion-lacking data again. Always open with a captivating story, and you'll immediately hook your listeners' brains emotionally, so much so that the data will actually mean something to them.

Storytelling needs constant practice, and the great news is that your story treadmill is always moving right along with you during the day. If you're at a party, and someone asks you, "How did you get into your line of work?" you'll now be able to answer that far more engagingly than before.

> *Being a great storyteller is an adventure. It's worth the time and investment to hone this craft because stories educate, inspire, connect, heal, and humanize.*

Let them hear you share the moments when you *knew* you *had* to do this work. Who was there? What was happening? How did you FEEL when it happened? What did you do about it? What was the outcome? Your experiences are unfolding because you walk this planet with a purpose to change the world a little bit, or a lotta bit, while you are here. So, tell your stories! Make note of experiences that you are currently living out. Write *Aha! Moments* down in a notebook or our journal, dedicated to story capture. Honor your own life experiences as your stories contribute to lifting up the world.

Let your own Story Fruition come out. Let all of your pertinent stories come out.
Tell them and tell them well!

—Melissa Reaves, Founder/CEO, Story Fruition, Sammamish, WA, 2022

Me: So, Gut Instinct, okay, you were.... right...AGAIN. Writing this book was important and really fun!

Gut Instinct: You're welcome. And, *always* remember...we're in this together.

Me: Promise?

Gut Instinct: Lying isn't our thing.

Me: I appreciate you.

Gut Instinct: Ditto, kid.

ABOUT THE AUTHOR

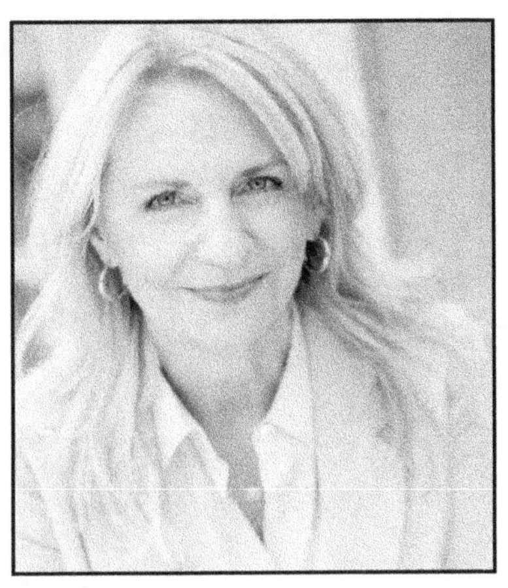

Melissa Reaves resides in Seattle, WA where she enjoys the beauty of the Pacific Northwest. She graduated with a Bachelor of General Studies from the University of Michigan/Ann Arbor, emphasizing her passions of theatre, marketing, journalism, and psychology—all which fit into her work today as an entrepreneur and storytelling mentor. She started acting at the ripe age of nine and has studied the art form of storytelling for over five decades. Melissa founded Story Fruition LLC and has been joyously mentoring executives all over the world on how to be captivating storytellers in their presentations, TEDx Talks, investor pitch presentations and boardroom meetings. In addition to storytelling for business applications, she is also a passionate storyteller for education and social advocacy. She speaks on Mental Health regarding OCD (Obsessive Compulsive Disorder), Transgender Rights and Diversity, Equity and Inclusion with her show, *Melanin Stories Matter*. She appears on *The Moth Stages, Risk Podcast, Ignite Seattle,* NPR, PBS's *STORIES FROM THE STAGE* and many international storytelling shows. Her work is known for rich characters and balanced infusions of humor with poignancy as she looks at her Life Journey and marvels in all the richness of it. She's the proud mother of her two kids, Quincy and Maisy; as well as Cat Mom to her two silver tabbies, Totoro and Thor.

If you are interested in learning how Story Fruition can help you or your organization, please drop us a line at **www.storyfruitioninfo.com** and we can book a complimentary thirty minute intro call. For more info: **www.StoryFruition.com**

Follow us!

Facebook: @storyfruition
LinkedIn: /company/story-fruition/
Instagram: story_fruition
Twitter: @StoryFruition
YouTube: Story Fruition

ACKNOWLEDGMENTS AND GRATITUDE

I want to thank so many wonderful people who have been on this journey with me both as a storyteller and as an entrepreneur. Your love, support, input, and sincere interest in making business storytelling a part of your lives is exciting, and I'm truly honored to be with you on it.

Thank you to my friends, clients, and fellow artists who have taught me the beauty of this craft and how we can take both personal and professional moments and weave them into compelling and captivating presentations, media interviews, and keynotes that spark audiences to lean in and listen to your stories. They matter. You matter.

So, thank you to:

Quincy Emerson for their fantastic cover design and watching them take that animation degree and exercise it fully for this book; Maisy Wagner and Lorane Matarazzo for listening to me endlessly talking about writing this book; Marla Schimke for knowing my sales and marketing career would be the set up for Story Fruition; Caleb Carr for sparking my interest to start my own company helping people be great storytellers like you showed us at Seattle University's Business Plan Competition; to Amelia Marckworth and the Seattle University Innovation & Entrepreneur Center for supporting my work with your students; Nick Hughes for accepting my tap on the shoulder at Hard Rock Café and inviting me to be your Seattle Pitch Coach; Kane Minkus and Sanjay Kumar for being my business advisors; Megan Lowes for your beautiful editing support and belief in this work; Lauren Archer, Greg Butcher, Bryan Brewer, Lisa L. Levy, and Stephanie Rogers for sharing feedback on the manuscript; Shiela Reaves and Olia Kazenina for your editing and contributions on the neuroscience of this work; Matthew Dicks for your own teaching and support in my storytelling skills; Jennifer Coburn for side coaching me in the publishing process; Paul Currington and Susan Fee for all your positive support since day one. Big gratitude to all the Melanin Stories Matter tellers and team. What beautiful shows we produced with purpose. Kent Whipple for being my first official storytelling teacher—you launched a rocket, didn't you, my beautiful and talented friend? And my A-team Publishers, Bridget Cook Burch, Rebecca Hall Gruyter, and Michael Beas, we are a fantastic team. And, last but certainly not least, my A-team at Story Fruition who help me every day to make sure the train stays on tracks: Thank you! Thank you!

To my weekly storytelling Master Mind group led by Sean Wellington and shared with Ronna Levy, Kory May, Andrew Shelffo, Richard Munchkin, Bob Dancer, Mary Jo Pollack, Neshama Franklin, Stephanie Rogers, Johanne Pelletier, Shweta Bhat, Danial Boyd, Cat Dean, Tracey Starin, Sharon Eisner, Kurt Mullen, Howard Lieberman, Carolyn Erickson, and the *ever-growing Swap Shop* "SWAPPERS"—thank you for helping me craft my own ninety-nine second or six-minute stories for shows!

To my clients who all contributed their beautiful stories in this book, thank you for opening up and daring to be vulnerable as you show the world your brilliance in business: Caleb Carr, Denise Cooper, Julia Cannell, Linda Fisk, Lisa Levy, Erin McCune, Tom Spann, Jung Suh, Erin McCune, Chris Jones, Phebe Rossi, Crystal Clenney, Pradnya Desh, The Korean Startup Center/Seattle, Juan Medina, Maria Luisa and the University of Washington-Tacoma, Sharon Podobnik, Dr. Noor Ali and Linda Fisk. Your stories inspire me and I'm grateful we've worked together. Thank you for sharing your journey!

And thank you to the entrepreneurs, leaders, and business visionaries who have dreams to better the world through your careers by becoming emotionally connected leaders. Whatever stage you are in, your stories matter, and I can't wait to hear how you're utilizing them to create worlds. You are deeply appreciated.

COVER ARTIST

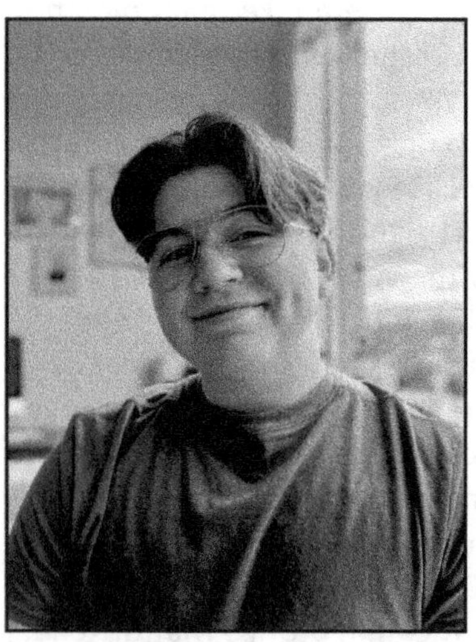

Quincy Emerson (they/them - he/him) is an animator residing in Portland, Oregon. They believe that animating is one of the most exciting art forms as it allows for unlimited creativity and expression. Quincy graduated top of their class from Laguna College of Art and Design with a BFA in animation and a minor in creative writing. Quincy has also worked as a storyboard artist and author of a children's workbook specializing in creative aerospace design. They enjoy baking cakes and playing with their cats in their downtime.

Instagram: @quincy.emerson

LinkedIn: https://www.linkedin.com/in/quincy-emerson-702059171/

RESOURCE PAGE

Website address: www.storyfruition.com
Book a 30 consultation: www.storyfruitioninfo.com
Free downloads: https://storyfruition.com/tools-%26-tips

REVIEWS

"Businesses have visions to improve the world. Tell that story clearly and you'll accelerate your success. This book, *The Storyteller's Mind Movie*, is the gas pedal for entrepreneurs."

—Kevin Harrington, Best Selling Author, CEO of TVGOODS.com, Original Shark on SHARKTANK

"If you are looking to increase your ability to influence people and impact their hearts and minds, this is the book for you. There is no more important skill to evolve than your ability to share your message and ideas in a way that creates inspiration, movement and engagement. This book will give you the most cutting-edge tools to do that."

—Kane Minkus, Founder/CEO of Industry Rockstars

"I've worked with Melissa Reaves for over fifteen years, and she has always emphasized the power of storytelling that bridges sales and marketing. Her approach to simplifying messaging so listeners feel emotionally connected to a business product or service is a game-changer. Unfortunately, the corporate world often forgets this—and it's imperative to create narratives that take our customers, partners, and internal teams on vivid emotional and transformational journeys. That's the power of storytelling. *The Storyteller's Mind Movie* is a book all sales and marketing teams and corporate leaders need to read and apply to their messaging."

—Marla Schimke, Head of Product Marketing, Broadcom

"I've known the power of storytelling in my own investor pitches – and to have this book now available for more entrepreneurs to shine in their own investor presentations is both welcomed and celebrated!"

—Caleb Carr, Founder/CEO/President, Vita Inclinata Technologies

"I have seen firsthand how Melissa's approach of leading with storytelling has improved the pitches of entrepreneurs preparing for everything from Seattle University's Harriet Stephenson Business Plan Competition to the Pegasus Startup World Cup, and the increased funding they get as a result. As investors, we remember your story longer than any pie chart, so entrepreneurs seeking capital raising need to read this smart and entertaining book. Your words and your visuals during an investor pitch are paramount. This book will help you stand out from the crowd so that your own business dreams come to fruition!"

—Amelia Marckworth, Director, Innovation & Entrepreneurship Center, Seattle University

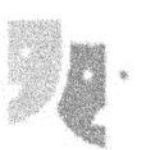

"*The Storyteller's Mind Movie* is terrific! It shows how to create human connection via story-telling in a fun, insightful and applicable way. It encourages you to self-reflect and become a better public speaker. The book guides you step by step to your storytelling crafting journey as you start to better understand the art and science behind it. Reading The Mind Movie book will inspire you to create your own story library that will benefit your personal and professional lives."

Olia Kazenina, CEO of Mind Pattern LLC

"*The Storyteller's Mind Movie* by Melissa Reaves is a consumable and highly impactful how-to craft and tell impactful stories. Melissa shares the key processes and demonstrates their power with stories from her clients. As readers, we see, hear and feel the experience! The book is wonderful. There are very few books I would ever re-read... this is a true tool and will always be close at hand."

Lisa L. Levy, Founder/CEO of Lcubed Consulting

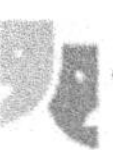

www.ingramcontent.com/pod-product-compliance
Lightning Source LLC
Chambersburg PA
CBHW081212130726
47997CB00009B/2640